Patricia Skinner

Studying Gender in Medieval Europe

Historical Approaches

First published 2018 by
PALGRAVE

Palgrave in the UK is an imprint of Macmillan Publishers Limited,
registered in England, company number 785998, of 4 Crinan Street,
London, N1 9XW.

Palgrave® and Macmillan® are registered trademarks in the United States,
the United Kingdom, Europe and other countries.

ISBN 978–1–137–38754–7 hardback
ISBN 978–1–137–38753–0 paperback

This book is printed on paper suitable for recycling and made from fully
managed and sustained forest sources. Logging, pulping and manufacturing
processes are expected to conform to the environmental regulations of the
country of origin.

A catalogue record for this book is available from the British Library.

A catalog record for this book is available from the Library of Congress.

*This book is dedicated to the memory of
my mother, Irene, a true feminist for whom no challenge
was insurmountable.*

Contents

Preface

This book owes its existence to all the 'foremothers' who have fought to hear medieval women's voices, and to promote gender equality and equity in the medieval academy. I want especially to acknowledge the friendship and guidance of Liesbeth van Houts, Jinty Nelson, Pauline Stafford, Liz Herbert McAvoy and Judith Bennett. Most of the book was written whilst working at Swansea University, where I have enjoyed the company of colleagues in the Centre for Gender, Culture and Society (GENCAS), and at the University of Winchester, where the Centre for Gender Studies hosts and celebrates interdisciplinarity. I am truly grateful for the feminist act that prompted both 'anonymous' reviewers to reveal their identities and engage with me whilst I made revisions, so thanks to Bronach Kane and particularly to Linda Mitchell for their generosity and time. The rewrite started at the extraordinary experience that is the Berkshire Conference for the History of Women and Gender in 2017, which celebrates inclusivity and is a model for how all academic conferences should be. Emily Cock made some crucial last-minute suggestions, and has been a valued colleague on the journey (especially on train rides) from draft to revision. If the revised version still has flaws, they are entirely of my own making.

If I'd known how hard it is to write a textbook, I might not have started this project, and I am now full of admiration for those who seem to do so effortlessly. That it has reached an end is entirely down to the support of my family. Thanks must also go to the team at Palgrave, particularly Rachel Bridgewater, who has been patiently waiting as deadline after deadline passed. I hope it's been worth the wait.

1

Setting the Scene

I am a medieval historian by training. I am a gender historian by inclina-
tion. At the start of my academic career in the 1980s, I found myself in
a minority in both fields: gender historians often worked in much later
periods, or preferred to think of themselves as women's historians. Very
few medieval historians specialized in gender, nor did they self-identify
as gender historians, for all that their work was gendered; some even
questioned the applicability of gender theory to medieval evidence, given
that medieval people 'didn't think about gender'. (But they *did* – they
just didn't articulate their thoughts in the same languages that modern,
academic theorists do.) This book is based loosely on an undergraduate
course that I taught from 1995 to 2007, which encouraged second-year/
sophomore students to try out the different theories and apply them to
sources that interested them. Even in that short time span, the proliferation of studies was both exciting and daunting. In the decade since then,
the landscape has changed still more, to the extent that it is possible to
compile anthologies of key readings as 'Companions' to gender history
(albeit that their coverage of the Middle Ages remains patchy). This
book is not a personal reflection. It starts its survey much earlier than the
1980s, but the acceleration and proliferation of work on gender during
the intervening decades will form a significant part of what follows.

Historiography books (books about *how* history has been written, and
current approaches to history-writing) often mirror the pattern of mutual
exclusion. Few of the, otherwise excellent, introductory textbooks on
Gender History mention the Middle Ages, let alone feature medieval examples. There are a number of – again, perfectly usable – textbooks introducing
students to Medieval History, but if women and/or gender feature in these,
it will often be as a bit of an afterthought, even well into the twenty-first

1

century (though gender historians have been involved in updating older works, for example Judith Bennett's revision of Warren Hollister's *Medieval Europe: A Short History*, now in its eleventh edition). The many excellent books that have been written about women and gender in the medieval world also tend to assume some prior knowledge of the period, which often leads to an omission of methodological or temporal framing. A substantial proportion of existing works has been written by scholars working in areas outside history departments, focusing in particular on later medieval literature in English and other languages, which adds another layer of complexity deriving from very different scholarly approaches (and an associated academic language that can be discipline-specific and difficult to follow for those untrained in the theoretical models that have become commonplace in English and other language studies). In each chapter of this book, therefore, words in **bold** are concepts which are further explained in the Glossary for each chapter. For experts in other fields than history, this book will come as a bit of a disappointment: although it will explore the impact of theory on gender history, it does not form the starting point in this survey, and I do not analyse medieval literary texts at all. There are plenty of works introducing students to Chaucer, or Marie de France, or Dante, or Arthurian romance. The exclusion of such works should not be taken as an indication that they have no value for the historian, however, and the themed Source Hunts in this book might provide a jumping-off point to explore this literary and creative world too. After all, medieval studies is an inherently – and necessarily – **interdisciplinary** field.

This book is, instead, written for a complete beginner in history, looking to find out about an approach – gender – that may be unfamiliar, and/or about a period that s/he has not studied before. For students that have already studied some gender history, some of the inspirational, 'classic' texts referred to here will be familiar, for medievalists have adopted many of their ideas and applied them to the medieval world. For students with some medieval history, this book offers ideas on how to expand beyond the standard narratives of kingdom formation, power, piety and authority, and think about how these might look if explored with a gendered eye. For hard-pressed members of staff/faculty, the book offers a frame and suggestions to guide students through both theoretical and primary materials, and the basis for dissertation or term paper topics.

The chapters are arranged thematically, and offer a guide to studying medieval gender history by combining three elements. First, each explores a particular theme and how it has been studied across over a century of academic work (within and outside the **academy** itself). The discussion within each chapter is organized roughly chronologically, but the book as a whole is not a history *of* gender. Each chapter suggests readings from 'classic' texts as well as more recent works: it is crucial to understand how successive generations of scholars have built upon, rejected or refined what came before. It is also important to recognize that gender history has its roots in work focused on women's neglected experiences and the ways in which women's voices have been ignored or suppressed, so in some chapters women will feature more heavily than men as topics such as bodies, regulation and identities are addressed. As we shall see, much early work on women and gender was obscured by their authors' inability to secure professional posts as historians, or by neglect of their work as 'marginal' to mainstream history. Some of the classics in gender history have absolutely nothing to say about the Middle Ages. My acid test for identifying such works as 'classics', however, is that they have provoked medievalists to test the applicability of their models on medieval material; retained their place on gender history syllabuses; and/or continue to be debated in scholarly conferences. Of course, that may be because their authors remain powerful figures in the academy, keen to ensure a legacy for successive students and thus perhaps revising their books for new readers; or that the publishers continue to re-issue such texts and restate their importance for commercial reasons, but neither of these explanations need devalue the actual influence of the works themselves.

Next, each chapter points towards a sample of medieval texts that can be profitably mined for information about the theme, and lend themselves to applying some of the theoretical approaches to reading the evidence itself – this is the Source Hunt. Many different types of text are represented here – chronicles, laws, charters, letters, biographies, to name just a few. With a more critical, *gendered* eye, it is soon apparent that much of the evidence used to reconstruct medieval social life was produced by an extraordinarily narrow sector of medieval society, white, male, clerical, and often elite. Rather than seeing this as a barrier, however, gender history equips scholars to take on this limited sample, and generates new and exciting questions about not only the authors, but also the social frameworks within which they worked. One chapter of this book, in fact, will also look specifically for works that were produced by women, but will ask whether female writers owed more to their social class than their gender: we cannot assume that the very articulate women of the medieval period whose writings are preserved a representative of women as a whole.

Finally, each chapter offers some suggestions for further reading, often by people who have adopted the approach discussed, or about the type of source we have explored. First, though, we need to set the scene.

Gender and No Medieval?

In the second decade of the twenty-first century, gender history still occupies a precarious position within the higher education systems of much of the developed world, and in some places is still entirely absent. In many history departments, it is still possible to find medieval history curricula with little or no gendered content, and the field as a whole lacks widespread institutional support, particularly from elite universities. Gender history had its origins in the struggle for social equality and women's **emancipation** in the late nineteenth and early twentieth centuries, a struggle that continues for women in many parts of the globe today, even in supposedly 'modern' nation states. For many gender historians, therefore, the modern (i.e. post-1800CE) fight by women (and some men) for social justice is at the core of their research, and current journals in the field are dominated by studies focusing on the modern era. The feminist journal *Signs*, for example, has only published one medieval article in its last ten issues, and other journals devoted to women's history, such as the *Journal of Women's History*, fare only slightly better. As medievalist Mathilde van Dijk has commented, the focus of women's historians on documenting 'ordinary' women has had the (perhaps unintended) effect of screening out the medieval era, where most texts document the lives of elites. In fact this statement can be nuanced somewhat as we reach the later Middle Ages, when records become fuller and more diverse in nature. Yet early work on women's history, driven by first-wave feminist movements of the later nineteenth century in Europe and the United States, and carried out largely by researchers working outside established university positions, regularly sought out the premodern origins of women's oppression, and thus laid the foundations for a gendered history that included much earlier periods. During the early twentieth century, approaches to history-writing itself diversified dramatically, with more interest in the social and economic conditions of the past and how patterns of power relations changed over time, or remained static over long periods. Medieval historians were at the forefront of this development, particularly in France, where 'total history' meant scrutinizing a much more diverse range of source materials, and examining social and cultural developments alongside political change. This in turn has given more room for the lives of women, and other neglected groups in the Middle Ages, to be explored in more detail.

The second-wave feminist movement of the 1960s and 1970s revived earlier questions about women's history in a self-consciously political way, often emphasizing the role of the education system in suppressing knowledge of earlier women's work and achievements, challenging the economic disempowerment of women and reclaiming control over women's bodies and sexuality. If first-wave feminism was thought to have had a narrow focus – the political emancipation of (certain) women – the second wave sought to broaden the agenda for action. Large and important books were written that sought to give a 'women's history of the world' or trace the distant origins and stubborn persistence of **patriarchal** systems that held women back in contemporary society. Yet again much of this work was very present-centred: in telling the story of women's 'progress' to emancipation, such histories either ignored the medieval era or moved swiftly on from it. Indeed, media coverage of modern examples of injustice or cruelty towards women often deploys the term 'medieval' to signal the backwardness (in their eyes) of the society under scrutiny. Very few historians have challenged this short-sightedness, with the major exception of Judith Bennett, whose articles and subsequent book-length study *History Matters* pointed up the benefits of taking a longer view and using the medieval period as a laboratory to test ideas about women's enduring subordinate status even as moments of change seemed to give them brief advances. Bennett's work will feature in more detail in the following chapters.

'Second-wave' feminism has come in for fierce criticism, however, particularly in the United States, for its perceived focus on white, middle-class, straight women's concerns. In 1989 law professor Kimberlé Crenshaw wrote what has become a foundational essay asking why Black women (her term) were 'theoretically erased' by a feminist theory that privileged whites and a race theory that privileged men. 'Demarginalizing the **intersection**' between the two fields, she sought to demonstrate how Black women were 'multiply burdened', and raise awareness of how tightly-defined identity politics (which we shall return to in Chapter 6) ignored the diversity of experiences *within* particular groups. Her ideas have influenced scholars in medieval studies, as we shall see, but did not draw as heavily upon historical perspectives.

A third wave of feminist activity emerged in the 1990s, fuelled and shaped by the rapid expansion (in academia, at least) of **postmodern** and **postcolonial** theory. The first emphasized the contingency and fluidity of ideas, whilst the second exposed the continued tendency in academic discussions and in public campaigns to assume, still, the concerns of white, straight, western men (and women) as an unproblematical norm. It explicitly criticized earlier feminist movements for not recognizing the variety of women's experiences conditioned by race, or class, or sexuality, or a combination of one or more of these factors, and rejected the idea of a single, overarching feminist movement that united all women in sisterhood. A collection of reprinted essays titled *Feminists Revision History* reflected the broader sweep that was now demanded, and explicitly included essays exploring race, class *and* gender. Yet newer work went further than simply broadening, and actively sought to discredit earlier work. In 2002 Becky Thompson suggested that the second wave had in fact represented a 'hegemonic feminism' that marginalized the voices and activism of women of colour. Crenshaw's term **intersectionality** – expressing precisely this awareness of more than one factor contributing to social exclusion or disempowerment – was being taken up by writers who sometimes misunderstood Crenshaw's original intent and made 'intersectional' an identity of its own.

Some media commentators now think a fourth wave of feminism is upon us, a product not so much of even newer ideas, but of the combination of third wave concerns with the explosion of internet-based media and communications that allow for multiple voices, campaigns, single-issue discussions and collective petitioning unimagined as recently as thirty years ago. The rise of social media offers an immediacy of commentary and criticism, and a set of campaigning tools, that connects communities across much of the developed world, but excludes those not networked in this way. The corollary to this is ever-increasing fragmentation, and often quite vicious arguments between groups and individuals who would self-identify as feminist, as well as a route for some opponents of feminist politics (including at least one distinguished medievalist) to voice misogynist views on their 'personal' websites that would be unacceptable in academic publications. Fourth wave also signals the disappointment of many women (and men) today that the issues of emancipation, sexual self-determination and economic oppression are still in need of addressing in many parts of the world, including those where most 'progress' is supposed to have been made. As Karen Offen has pithily observed, it is possible to have 'success without impact'.

We shall return to feminism as an identity in more detail in Chapter 6, below, but it is worth pausing briefly here to think about the 'wave' analogy that I have just used, which as we can see is not without controversy. All of these 'waves' might be considered to impose their own, tyrannous framework on the study of women and gender based only on political developments in the United Kingdom and United States. They leave swathes of the twentieth century without any apparent feminist activity (academic or otherwise), which is clearly nonsensical. They also encourage a partitioning-off and devaluing of earlier work as so full of shortcomings that it can be safely ignored. In her thoughtful introduction to a set of essays exploring feminism in the United States, Nancy Hewitt comments that 'third-wave' essay collections 'often focus on setting young feminists apart from their predecessors'. This rupture between generations of historians is nothing new, but the presentist agenda in much of the debate, it could be argued, is one reason for gender's slow progress into academic maturity and its neglect of longer viewpoints.

In 1986 the *American Historical Review* published Joan Scott's influential article 'Gender: a useful category of historical analysis'. To those committed to women's and/or feminist history, 'gender' presented itself as both affirmation and challenge. What were the advantages of adopting a gendered outlook over continuing with a focus on women? Was gender simply a means of effacing the strident feminism of women's history, making it in some way more 'acceptable' to academic study? In fact, as the editors of the new *Gender and History* journal pointed out in 1989, the history of relations between the sexes, highlighted by women's history, could be used as a means to explore other, unequal power relations, and to demonstrate that women could be the oppressors as well as the oppressed. 'Sisterhood' and Eileen Power's phrase 'rough and ready equality' (on which more later), viewed in this light, began to look somewhat idealistic approaches to the medieval evidence.

The transition from women's to gender studies in academia, which was patchy, uneven and by no means unproblematic, is exemplified by two books of essays edited by Mary Erler and Maryanne Kowaleski in 1988 and 2003: both dealt with 'power', but the approaches of their contributors demonstrate the changes in the fifteen years separating their publication (and both the editors and Jo Ann McNamara's essay in the second volume explicitly outlined how the field had shifted). In the first volume, the contributors aimed simply to explore definitions of power as they played out in male-female relations, and how women might exploit alternative routes to influence and express their power indirectly, as wives, literary patrons, peasant entrepreneurs and saints. Further original interpretations of power appear in a major conference held in Brussels in 1996, which explored 'Women and the Powers of Women in Byzantium and the West'. We might note in that plural 'powers' – again the contributors ranged across varieties of power-wielding including marriage, queenship, becoming a nun, legal frameworks, patronage and motherhood. In some ways, therefore, the transition to gender never really forgot the centrality of women, and the Byzantinists Angeliki Laiou and Evelyne Patlagean (in her early work, see Appendix) foregrounded the family, economic resources and power in their work.

By 2003, as Erler and Kowaleski acknowledged, the intellectual landscape had changed considerably. They pinpoint the influence of philosophers Michel Foucault and Judith Butler, both of whom emphasized that power relations and gendered roles were essentially constructed products of social **discourse**, requiring 'performance' and ultimately less about individual agency. 'Women' as a category had become problematic, as it seemed to claim a universal female experience that had never really existed. The focus now was less on recovering the realities of women's power and more on how it was represented (or not) in language and text. Thus gender historians' responsibility was to expose and challenge the 'master narrative', in particular the way in which the patriarchal concerns of many medieval texts had shaped a limited picture of medieval culture focusing on the political and institutional. 'Gendering' had already become a verb, used to describe this process of exposure, and was used to great effect in a series of essays published as a special issue of *Gender and History* in 2000, all of which, to a greater or lesser extent, confronted the ways in which female *and* male gender roles were constructed and represented in different types of text.

The key element to gendered readings was to understand that gender itself was a **relational** category: it explored its subject in relation to others, and recognized that the changing context might also change the status or abilities of an individual to have agency at all. Gender relations did not remain fixed over time: at an individual level, too, gender relations could be fluid as a person progressed through different stages of life, gaining and losing authority directly related to age, activities and relationships. Power could come and go. Gendered readings of medieval texts, therefore, were and are highly conscious of not only what is presented on the page, but how it came to be presented in that way – what concerns, unwritten norms, personal relationships and issues of patronage shape the account being written. These questions take on additional importance when applied to the silences and inconsistencies of medieval texts.

Medieval and No Gender?

If gender history has had some trouble accommodating the Middle Ages (and I realize this is a sweeping claim that will gradually be unpicked in the chapters that follow, not to mention challenged by reviewers of this book), generations of medieval historians have blithely overlooked or even consciously ignored women and gender in their analyses. As history-writing became professionalized in the late nineteenth century, its focus was on the privileged fields of political and national history-writing, and historians trained in that period celebrated the 'scientific' approach to the past that claimed to remove the historian's own views almost entirely. The historical and political worlds did of course intersect – many (mostly male) politicians have written history, and professional historians (mostly male) have long advised politicians (and the History and Policy group in the United Kingdom still advocates such collaboration) – but that did not mean that history could be overtly 'political', that is, have an agenda to campaign for social change.

Keith Jenkins has usefully drawn a distinction between History (with an upper-case H) – the professional field, preserving its boundaries and practices and hiding behind a protestation of detached, scientific judgement to select only that which is held to be significant – and history (lower case), the sum of human past experience, much of which has been ignored and overlooked. Jenkins is sceptical of reaching another person's past *on their terms* – historians cannot detach themselves from present concerns, thus the claims of History to represent the most plausible version of the past – a 'master narrative' to which we shall return – are effectively dead. Whilst not explicitly engaging with feminism (Jenkins later collaborated with his colleague Sue Morgan to put this right), formulations such as this provide the space for alternative histories to emerge, and legitimize history-writing as a form of activism (as also espoused by the triennial Berkshire Conference on the History of Women, Genders and Sexualities). Yet there is still much resistance to this viewpoint.

In relation to the Middle Ages, much eighteenth and nineteenth century historiographical energy centred around the discovery and collation of medieval texts, and their publication in scholarly editions. These large-scale projects, several of which, including the English *Rolls* series, the German *Monumenta Historicae Germanica* (which, given the fact that it documents the rise of empire, covers much of France and northern Italy as well) and the Italian *Fonti per la Storia d'Italia*, are still going strong, were motivated by nationalist ideals of the origins and longevity of nation states, and the focus was on the formation of political society – kings, councils and parliaments, law and diplomacy. If women featured at all in the narratives that resulted, it was to cement such institutions through high-level marriages, or to feature as entirely exceptional oddities (female rulers, prominent saints). As we shall see later on in Chapter 5, the editorial focus of such projects actually hid a lot of medieval women from view.

Ironically, the publishing of medieval legal texts within these collections provided substantial material for early campaigners to challenge women's exclusion from certain rights, such as the right to maintain control of their own property on marriage. Writing histories that highlighted and undermined the historical justification for political and social inequality, however, directly challenged the nineteenth century ideal of objectivity and professionalism. The burgeoning academy largely excluded women from its members, and thus suppressed – often through indifference – much of the work done in this field. Angelika Epple and Angelika Schaser have termed this a 'metaphorical death'. Yet as recent, feminist-inspired scholarship is beginning to reveal, women wrote large-scale and ambitious histories (see below, especially Chapter 5), and the editions of many of the core medieval texts with which we now work were in fact prepared by, or involved the labour of, women. They were either not credited at all, or listed as 'assistants' to the male editors, and it is clear that **misogyny** played a large part in the final editorial decisions. Kathryn Maude has drawn attention to some of these hidden scholars, pointing out that students' access to medieval texts is still dominated by editions produced in this era of masculine authority. And the problem does not stop at editions: translated sources in the multi-volume *English Historical Documents* are also subject to editorial interventions. The now often used will of the Anglo-Saxon noblewoman Wulfwaru, reproduced in volume I of this august series (published in 1955), is prefaced by a comment from Dorothy Whitelock, its translator, that this is a document of a 'woman of no historical importance'. Of course, the *inclusion* of the will as an exemplar subtly works against Whitelock's claim – and this may of course have been her intention. Certainly the comment remains in the second edition of the work, published in 1979.

There are two broad exceptions to this story of exclusion and neglect. Early work on Christian history could not ignore the central role that women's piety and spirituality played in the expansion of the early Church, albeit that their participation and authority became increasingly circumscribed as the Church matured and drew selectively on biblical precedent to establish male privilege and leadership. Major publications such as the multi-volume *Acta Sanctorum* (*AASS*, from 1643 to 1940), *Patrologia Latina* (*PL*, from 1844 onwards) and *Patrologia Graeca*

(PG from 1857 onwards) all collected texts relating to the early Church (*PL* and most of the *AASS* in the west, *PG* and a limited number of lives in the *AASS* in the east). Although male writers and saints outnumber female in all three collections, they nevertheless provided a place for early research into women's lives.

Gendered patterns of exclusion from Latin education in the Middle Ages (to which we shall return) also saw women pioneering writing in vernacular languages from the twelfth century onwards, making them from the start a prime subject for research into medieval language and literature, much of which was done by female scholars who might similarly have been excluded from a classical education giving them access to Latin. These medievalist **foremothers** are only now getting the credit they deserve. A good place to start looking for biographies of some of these women (a form of '**recovery history**'), is the colossal catalogue compiled by Jane Chance, *Women Medievalists and the Academy*, published in 2005, and featuring over seventy scholars, including some autobiographical reflections by those still living and active at that date. This is by no means a comprehensive study, as Chance herself admits, and favours scholarship in the United States, omitting several prominent European scholars and those who publish/ed in languages other than English. The list here can usefully be supplemented by various national and international biographical dictionaries, some of which are now retrospectively working on increasing the representation of women among their subjects. Yet what is striking about many of the biographies is the fact that many of the women featured grew up in already quite privileged circumstances, often in academic or religious households, and had – or were given – space to develop their scholarly interests, and/or pursued those interests outside traditional academic career paths.

The study of medieval history has diversified along with history-writing as a whole in the past century, and a broad range of views on women, feminism and gender can be found represented among medievalists, albeit as a minority in each field. Patrick Geary suggested in 1994 that American medievalists had had a leading role in putting gender history into medieval studies across the globe, and pointed up the contrast (which was even greater before the advent of global web-based communications) between European and American medieval scholarship practices. Yet whilst it is true that many of the theoretical texts highlighted in this book were produced by American scholars, Geary somewhat underplays existing trends in European historiography of the twentieth century that laid the ground for a more receptive and gendered medieval history. It was medievalists, for example, who developed and engaged most enthusiastically with the *Annales* idea of 'total history', emerging in France from the 1920s onwards. The historians in this group, and those whom they trained, rather than focusing on a definition of politics, turned to other disciplines including the social sciences to explore social history, using statistics (albeit imperfect sets) to explore long-term continuities and changes in society. It is fair to say that early *Annales* work was not tremendously concerned with women as a group, but later historians trained within this tradition, such as Christiane Klapisch-Zuber, would demonstrate the power of the total history approach when focusing on gender issues. The advent of computers in the academy assisted still further in this 'serial' approach, enabling Klapisch-Zuber and US scholar David Herlihy to publish large-scale studies based on collecting and collating what might now be termed 'big data' (and today would be considerably 'bigger', given the power of electronic searches).

Moreover, the relatively supportive environment of the UK London School of Economics (LSE) in the same period produced a generation of female scholars and important work on women's lives in the medieval and early modern periods, turning away from grand narratives of history to focus on the social and economic lives of those further down the social scale. They thus preceded the influential group of Marxist historians in the United Kingdom in the 1950s and 1960s, who focused on workers and peasants in medieval society (but were less interested in gender), and opened up the way (albeit unconsciously) for other **subaltern** groups to be studied in greater depth. Again, early work by feminist historians pointed to the ways in which a focus on *class* meant that *gender* was ignored, thus foreshadowing Crenshaw's articulation of intersection.

Although medieval gender history still faces challenges – ultimately, gender in its broadest sense should underpin *all* medieval history, and not need to exist as a separate category – it now has strong advocates across the world. The Society for Medieval Feminist Scholarship, now in its fourth decade (or third in its current form), champions and publishes not only new work in medieval studies, but also campaigns on issues of prejudice and exclusion within and outside the modern academic world. Yet with the death or retirement of many pioneers of the 1970s and 1980s, it is important to ensure their legacy is not simply to be recognized as 'foremothers', but also to build on and utilize their foundational work to ask new and risky questions, and to continue to challenge an academic culture where traditional medieval history – about state-building, conflict, crusade, patterns of power – is still so dominant in textbook narratives, and 'gender' is equated far too often with 'women'. As Judith Bennett points out, 'Hate them we might, but we also have to concede [textbooks'] power, especially their power over how women are remembered in history'. This textbook eschews a narrative history of the Middle Ages and instead offers a guide to approaching what can sometimes seem a rather distant era through a series of thematic chapters. In the last chapter of the book the inherent interdisciplinarity now visible in medieval studies, and the implications this might have for future 'historical' approaches, will be explored.

Definitions

I have so far discussed 'women and gender' together, but we need to be more precise at this point: 'gender history' became popular as a term in the late twentieth century (the 1980s and 1990s), but it drew upon and developed the two earlier waves of feminist history-writing already highlighted. It is thus frequently conflated with 'women' (I have probably been as guilty of this confusion as others in my previous writing). I therefore want to make a distinction between women's history, feminist history and gender history in this book, with which readers may disagree: I do not claim that these are hard and fast categories, and there is some blurring at the boundaries, but they do explain why women feature so heavily in a book about 'gender', and they do reflect the ways in which categories were used before 'gender' entered academic language. So:

- I use 'women's history' to refer to the history *of* women, frequently written *by* women, and motivated by a desire to restore women to the historical panorama; it is often limited simply to documenting women, rather than drawing broader analytical conclusions. Broadly speaking, it does little to change what historians think of as 'significant'.

- By 'feminist history', I indicate work that has not only documented and restored women to historical narratives, but has *used* that knowledge to make wider claims to political and social (and academic) equality in the historian's own time. Thus *some* women's history was also feminist in its aims, in particular in terms of its aspiration to reshape the historical frame beyond an 'add women and stir' approach. Such history-writing often consciously or unconsciously exposes some of the inequalities still present in the higher education system. As we have seen, however, 'feminism' itself has become ever harder to define.

- 'Gender history' is broader in scope than either of these two categories, drawing the lessons learnt from gender inequalities and applying them to wider issues of **disempowerment**. It is therefore often still inherently political, and thus for gender historians, women's history does not go far enough. Controversially, though, gender encompasses the study of women *and* men, and explores masculinities as a sub-field. Some feminist historians would not see themselves as gender historians.

These categories are not set in stone, and historians often move between them as they publish new work. Gender historians see their field as open and inclusive, but sometimes do not self-identify as feminists – or, indeed, as gender historians at all. Yet much history published as 'gender history' is in fact still 'women's history', and the history of power relations in the past, even in a solely male environment, can be thought of as gender history even if its authors do not consciously embrace that term. Early histories of masculinity are good examples of how more traditional historians have entered the world of gender, with varying degrees of success. Gender history has essentially reclaimed early women's history, some of which was explicitly feminist in its aims, and some gender historians have feminist objectives in their work, but not all feminist historians accept gender as an appropriate label for their work. In particular, the institutional acceptance of gender history within the academy, it is argued, has distanced the field from its radical, political origins. Some feminists see gender as a safe, *de*-politicized field that legitimates and re-establishes male-dominated concerns and discourses. Further, the development of masculinity as a thriving field within gender studies is sometimes cited as 'restoring male dominance through the back door'. Others argue that it is up to gender historians to remain radical and relevant. Anna Krylova, for example, has recently argued that gender still deals mainly in the male/female **binary**, embedding assumptions that it should be unpicking, such as the hierarchy of values. She prefers the term **dichotomy**, which still expresses difference but is not necessarily limited to just two categories and does not crystallize existing imbalances of value or power. Only time will tell whether her argument, drawn from feminist philosophy and using modern case studies as illustrations, will gain broader acceptance.

Thus as we navigate through the development of the different ways of studying women and gender in the past, it is important to be aware that the labels used are themselves the subject of controversy amongst scholars. There is no 'right' answer – unsettling perhaps, but it makes for a field that is dynamic and welcoming to new voices and views.

History-writing is essentially opinion based on evidence. History students are exposed relatively early in their syllabuses to debates surrounding the possibility (or not) of ever reaching historical 'truth' and 'fact'. (Students in other disciplines reading this book might have to take this point on trust.) The impact of postmodern thought on history in the 1990s challenged the idea that there can be any one, authoritative or 'right' version of history, as every historian is a product of her/his surroundings, with individual agendas. That is not to say that all resulting versions of the past presented in their histories are equally valid: the important test case involving David Irving and his portrayal of the Holocaust, played out in the UK courts in 2000, centred around his flawed historical methodology rather than his abhorrent views. Yet history-writing has changed radically in the twentieth and early twenty-first centuries, responding (and contributing) to political movements. This is a long way from the tightly focused, 'scientific' history of the late nineteenth century academy. It is important to recognize that medieval history has shed much of its self-assurance about reading medieval texts as 'evidence'. Whatever the merits of postmodern thought for modern history, there is no doubt that medieval history has benefited from tapping into a theory that allows for uncertainties and possibilities alongside known – or perhaps better, agreed-upon – 'facts'. Arguably, it has refreshed the discipline and turned attention to alternative interpretations and readings. One huge area of growth has been the rise in the study of how the modern era has engaged with and recreated the medieval period in what Umberto Eco termed 'neomedievalism', the study of modern culture's appropriation of medieval themes (which as I write in 2017 has manifested itself in medieval symbols being used by far-right groups to peddle their repugnant, white supremacist views), which he contrasts with 'responsible philological examination', that is, medieval history more traditionally understood. (Far-right groups aside, medievalism more broadly offers useful and usable linkages between a past that can seem very distant, and a present that sometimes does not feel so 'modern'.) It has also demanded that historians take a hard look at their own assumptions as they work. Historians in medieval studies still seek to determine and describe a picture of past society that is supported by the documentary or material evidence in front of them, but the range of histories that can now be written no longer needs to adhere to a set idea of what 'proper' history – or History – is. Medievalists often have rather less evidence to go on than their modernist colleagues anyway, but have participated fully in these developments, and gender history has been at the forefront of changing ideas about how we – as historians, students, public – view the past.

The themes chosen for each chapter reflect, as far as is possible, the concerns of early and contemporary gender historians. Chapter 2 sets out why a sense of the medieval past is crucial to modern studies of gender, not least because 'medieval' has such varying applications as a term, both negative and unenlightened but also positive and utopic. Chapter 3 explores medieval understandings of 'Bodies'. In a contemporary world where physical, biological sex no longer determines a person's chosen (or assigned) gender, it actually becomes easier to understand theories that envisaged just one sex continuum, with men and women placed along its length, and the competing view of two separate sexes that supplanted these ideas. Medical texts may not be reliable guides to medical practice on the ground, but they do transmit ancient and medieval ideas about bodies that fed into later justifications

for gender hierarchy. Chapter 4, 'Rules', therefore, focuses on these justifications in the form of religious and secular laws, the rules that were
preached, written down and imperfectly enforced, and how these crystallized gender roles along binary lines. Alongside laws and religious
regulation, less formal sets of rules enshrined in conduct books of the
later Middle Ages are also considered. The authority evident in such
projects is explored further in Chapter 5, where I focus on women's
'Voices' and how these expose compliance with, and resistance to, the
male-dominated authorial norm. At least one of the writers featured,
Christine de Pizan (d. 1430), has been called the first 'feminist', even
if Christine herself might not have recognized such a label. Chapter 6,
therefore, confronts the thorny issue of 'Identities', bringing us full
circle to a discussion of how modern identity politics – gendered, sexual,
ethnic, queer – have shaped major contributions to medieval gender
history. Chapter 7 speculates on how a gendered approach has opened
the way to queer readings that might in time reshape what medieval
historians consider to be 'important', and offers some suggestions for
future research priorities.

Of course, one person's 'key theme' might not be another's – I have
already set out some of the parameters which shape this particular
textbook. And gender history is not static: some authors that we shall
be looking at, for example Judith Bennett and John Boswell, later
revisited some of their earlier essays to reflect on developments in the
field, but the 'originals' are also cited here in order to show how they
contributed to contemporary debates. Also important is the growing
phenomenon of self-publishing: many activists in the field are no
longer willing to submit to the power politics of academia's anonymous peer review, and then wait nearly a year to see their papers in
print, and the reading lists for this book include some of the sharpest
online blog entries from emerging voices who will no doubt set new
agendas. I do not list blogs per se, however, because they often have
limited shelf lives, and many are quite superficial in their engagement
with medieval culture.

How you eventually decide to read these and the more traditional
books and articles, and in what order, is entirely up to you – this is not a
prescriptive 'how to do medieval gender history' textbook, more a rough

guide to what's out there at the time of writing (2017), and an invitation to join the exploration of a dynamic, constantly engaging field. There has never been a better time to go source-hunting, with rich, online resources in their original languages and/or English translation available from many university and national repositories, so use this book as a waymarker, and enjoy the journey.

Key Reading: Journals

American Historical Review, founded 1895, key article:

Joan Scott, 'Gender: a useful category of historical analysis', *AHR*, 91 (1986), 1053–1075.

Gender and History, founded 1989, edited by a collective. Throughout its life it has featured historiographical articles on 'Foremothers', several of whom were/are medievalists.

Historical Reflections/Réflexions Historiques, founded 1974. Has strong representation of gender and medieval articles.

Journal of Feminist Studies in Religion, founded 1985. Features important articles on gender and spirituality in the Middle Ages.

Journal of Gender Studies, founded 1991. Aims to publish interdisciplinary work, and has published several influential position pieces on the history of gender and medieval studies: see Kathryn Maude's essay, 'Citation and marginalisation: the ethics of feminism in Medieval Studies', in volume 23.3 (2014), 247–261.

Journal of Medieval History, has frequently published articles on gender since its first issue in 1975.

Journal of Women's History, founded 1989 in the United States. Volume 26.1, published in 2014, devoted most of the issue to remembering the late Gerda Lerner, pioneer of feminist studies.

Medieval Feminist Forum: A Journal of Gender and Sexuality (formerly *Medieval Feminist Newsletter*), founded 1986. Journal of the Society for Medieval Feminist Scholarship.

The Medieval Globe; The Medieval History Journal; Medieval Worlds: these three titles are discussed in Chapter 2.

Nashim: A Journal of Jewish Women's Studies and Gender Issues, founded in 1998, has a mix of medieval and modern articles and numerous special issues.

Parergon: Bulletin of the Australian and New Zealand Association for Medieval and Renaissance Studies, established in 1971 and strong on gender and interdisciplinary work.

Past and Present, founded in 1952, has always had a strong medieval content, and publishes Viewpoints alongside research articles.

Signs: A Journal of Women in Culture and Society, founded 1975. Its virtual issue, *Signs@40*, is a useful guide to the theoretical frameworks which have evolved over the past 40 years: http://signsat40.signsjournal.org.

Speculum, the journal of the Medieval Academy of America, publishing since 1926. See Judith Bennett's commentary on its ambiguous title in her 1993 article 'Medievalism and feminism' in the same journal, vol. 68.2 (1993).

Viator: Medieval and Renaissance Studies

Women's History Review, founded 1992 in the United Kingdom. Volume 1 is online with free access.

Source Hunts: Online and Print Resources

British Library: The BL's Digitised Manuscripts site offers texts from across medieval Europe: www.bl.uk/manuscripts/.

Other museum websites, such as the Fitzwilliam in Cambridge, the Ashmolean in Oxford, Metropolitan Museum of Art in New York, and the Walters Art Museum in Baltimore feature highlights of their collections online.

English Historical Documents is a series published by Cambridge University Press and has four volumes covering the period 500–1485, including translated excerpts of legal texts.

Dumbarton Oaks: The Dumbarton Oaks Center has numerous online resources to support Byzantine Studies, including its Bibliography on

Women and Gender, its Hagiography Database, its Catalog of Byzantine Seals and its guide to printed translations of Byzantine saints' lives, all linked from www.doaks.org/research/byzantine/resources

Epistolae: Medieval Women's Letters at Columbia University, United States: https://epistolae.ccnmtl.columbia.edu.

The Internet Medieval Sourcebook: Core to source hunting are three linked websites that were developed in the 1990s as a collaborative effort to put translated source materials online, hosted at Fordham University, New York. The sites consisted of material specially translated for the Sourcebooks, plus links to the websites of academics who had allowed their own translations to be included and made accessible. At the time of writing, the Sourcebooks are still functioning reasonably well, though some of those external links have broken, either because the materials they led to have since been published in textbooks, or the academic concerned has moved institution, or, in a few cases, because putting the material online had breached copyright laws. There are now more, and more sophisticated, collections of online medieval source materials, but nothing so extensive as the Sourcebooks:

http://legacy.fordham.edu/halsall/sbook.asp.

The Internet Women's History Sourcebook
http://legacy.fordham.edu/halsall/women/womensbook.asp.

People with a History: an Online Guide to LGBT History
http://legacy.fordham.edu/Halsall/pwh/index-med.asp#c5.

Feminae: Feminae is a substantial bibliographical resource indexing work on medieval women, sexuality and gender studies. It does not appear to have been updated since 2008, but remains an invaluable resource for starting off a literature search:

https://inpress.lib.uiowa.edu/feminae/WhatIsFeminae.aspx.

History of Architecture: Site at Columbia University has a medieval section:

www.mcah.columbia.edu/ha/html/medieval.html

Index of Christian Art: Site at Princeton University https://ica.princeton. edu is a subscription-only site, but with an accessible front page of images. Check if your institution subscribes.

The Jewish Women's Archive includes contributions by scholars of medieval Jewish history on family, medicine and other themes, including translated texts:

http://jwa.org.

Medieval Writings on Secular Women, ed. P. Skinner and E. van Houts (London: Penguin, 2011). Created to provide a wide range of source excerpts in English translation in an affordable form for students.

The Portable Antiquities Scheme: A searchable database of finds by metal detectorists in the United Kingdom, many still to be catalogued or described:

www.finds.org.uk.

Further Reading

J. Bennett, *History Matters: Patriarchy and the Challenge of Feminism* (Philadelphia, PA: University of Pennsylvania Press, 2006).
J. Bennett, *Medieval Europe: a Short History* (11th edition New York: McGraw-Hill, 2010).
A Companion to Gender History, ed. T. Meade and M. Wiesner-Hanks (Oxford: Wiley-Blackwell, 2003).
K. Crenshaw, 'Demarginalizing the intersection of race and sex: a black feminist critique of antidiscrimination doctrine, feminist theory and antiracist politics', *University of Chicago Legal Forum*, 1 (1989), article 8, online at: http://chicagounbound.uchicago.edu/cgi/viewcontent.cgi?article=1052&context=uclf.

U. Eco, 'Dreaming the Middle Ages', in his *Travels in Hyperreality*, tr. W. Weaver (New York: Harcourt Brace, 1986).

The Feminist History Reader, ed. Sue Morgan (London: Routledge, 2006).

Feminists Revision History, ed. A.-L. Shapiro (New Brunswick, NJ: Rutgers UP, 1994).

P. Geary, 'Visions of medieval studies in North America', in *The Past and Future of Medieval Studies*, ed. J. van Engen (Notre Dame, IN and London: University of Notre Dame Press, 1994), 45–57.

Gender and Historiography: Studies in the History of the Earlier Middle Ages Honour of Pauline Stafford, ed. J. L. Nelson and S. Reynolds with S. M. Johns (London: IHR, 2012). Now open access at http://humanities-digital-library. org/index.php/hdl/catalog/book/genderandhistoriography.

Gender, Language and the Periphery, ed. J. Abbou and F. H. Baider (Amsterdam: John Benjamins, 2016).

Gendering Historiography: Beyond National Canons, ed. A. Epple and A. Schaser (Frankfurt and New York: Campus Verlag, 2009).

Gendering the Master Narrative: Women and Power in the Middle Ages, ed. M. Erler and M. Kowaleski (Ithaca, NY: Cornell University Press, 2003).

Gendering the Middle Ages, ed. P. Stafford and A. Mulder-Bakker, Special Issue of *Gender and* History, 12.3 (2000), subsequently published in book form (Oxford: Blackwell, 2001).

K. Jenkins, *Re-Thinking History* (London: Routledge, 1991).

A. Krylova, 'Gender binary and the limits of poststructuralist method', *Gender and History*, 28.2 (2016), 307–323.

A. Laiou, *Women, Family and Society in Byzantium* (Aldershot: Ashgate, 2011).

J. A. McNamara, 'Women and power through the family revisited', in *Gendering the Master Narrative: Women and Power in the Middle Ages*, ed. M. C. Erler and M. Kowaleski (Ithaca, NY and London: Cornell University Press, 2003), 17–30.

No Permanent Waves: Recasting Histories of U.S. Feminism, ed. N. A. Hewitt (New Brunswick: Rutgers University Press, 2010).

K. Offen, 'Writing the history of feminism (old and new): impacts and impatience', in *The Women's Liberation Movement: Impacts and Outcomes*, ed. Kristina Schulz (Bern: Berghahn, in press 2017).

The Oxford Handbook of Women and Gender in Medieval Europe, ed. J. Bennett and R. Mazo Karras (Oxford: Oxford University Press, 2013).

Saints, Scholars and Politicians: Gender as a Tool in Medieval Studies (Studies in Honour of Anneke Mulder-Bakker), ed. M. van Dijk and R. Nip (Turnhout: Brepols, 2005).

M. Sauer, *Gender in Medieval Culture* (London: Bloomsbury, 2015).

B. Thompson, 'Multi-racial feminism: recasting the chronology of second-wave feminism', *Feminist Studies*, 28.2 (2002), 336–360.

Women Medievalists and the Academy, ed. Jane Chance (Madison: The University of Wisconsin Press, 2005).

Women and Power in the Middle Ages, ed. M. C. Erler and M. Kowaleski (Athens, GA: University of Georgia Press, 1988).

Glossary

academy	The community of scholars working in institutions such as universities, producing (and controlling) knowledge about the past
Annales	See discussion in Chapter 2
binary	Two distinct categories in opposition to each other
CE	'Common era' dating – see Chapter 2
dichotomy	Possibility of divergence into two or more categories
discourse	A dominant or accepted set of views that nevertheless is subject to challenge and change
disempowerment	Being excluded from social, cultural or economic opportunity on the basis of rules or norms set up by the dominant social group
emancipation	Narrowly speaking, women's right to vote in political elections; more broadly, their right to make their own decisions freely over issues concerning their lives
foremothers	Female historians whose work may or may not have influenced subsequent generations, pioneers
interdisciplinary	Studying a subject from multiple approaches, for example combining history, literary studies, anthropology, etc., to produce a richer picture than single-discipline work
intersectionality	The realization that gender is only one category, and that analysis needs to take into account its combination with other categories such as race, colour, religious belief, sexuality, impairment and disability

misogyny	Literally, 'hatred of women', but more generally any action that is consciously or unconsciously repressive towards women
patriarchal	Putting the interests of 'fathers' – by definition male – first. For more on patriarchy see Chapter 4
postcolonial	An approach that recognizes and challenges 'western' dominance of descriptions and interactions with subject peoples, emerging from modern, decolonizing nations but being applied to earlier periods
postmodern/ist	Rejecting the certainty of modernity, that we have 'arrived' at a final answer for everything
recovery history	Rescuing subjects from obscurity, largely a documenting exercise
relational	Not fixed, responding to and shaped by other conditions
subaltern	Any subjected or oppressed individual or group, particularly in colonial contexts, e.g. British-ruled India, Spanish or Portuguese Latin America, Italian or French-ruled African states

2

Why 'Medieval' Matters
to Gender History

We touched above on the early role of medieval historians to provide explanations for the origins and growth of state structures, and the ways in which record series were published in national, scholarly editions to support this project. History has therefore developed as a discipline along national lines, and looks very different in its emphases depending on region. This has had a knock-on effect on gender history, which has also developed very differently. Gender historians recognize this, and have tried to break down barriers by collaborating on edited volumes with titles such as *Gendering Historiography: beyond National Canons* (2009, see Chapter 1) and *Making Women's Histories: beyond National Perspectives* (2013). Yet that word 'beyond' in both titles, and the fact that the contents of each of these books are still essentially reports from individual, nation-based perspectives, suggests that the editors in each case still see national perspectives as a starting point, and *countering* these through a more nuanced gender history as an impossible project. This is partly due to the lack of chronological depth in both works – neither explores the world *before* the advent of the modern nation state, as medieval feminists have begun to do, to see how and when (and if) women really were excluded from the national project.

Gender history, for the most part, remains a nationally segmented field. The sheer variety of histories that 'gender' is used to describe presents difficulties when trying to present a usable summary of the state of the field. This has led some medieval scholars to write books that have wide-ranging titles but which, very early on in their texts, narrow down their focus to quite limited ranges of evidence (an example, that explicitly defended its position as part of a broader spectrum of studies, was the modern-focused *Gender and History: Retrospect and Prospect*). This book is called *Studying Gender in Medieval Europe*. In the global community of the twenty-first century, it might be asked why it is not broader, widening its scope to the study of gender in the Americas before the sixteenth century, or medieval India, or Africa, or the rich and complex histories of China and Japan. But this is a textbook about studying the idea of gender and applying it to medieval European source materials, not a history *of* medieval Europe. Experts in those global regions will no doubt already be familiar with the 'classic' texts as they relate to their own areas of expertise, or have alternative 'classics' to suggest to their students (Gail Hershatter and Wang Zheng usefully highlighted points of comparison and difference for Chinese history in an article of 2008). Europe itself presents challenges too: sources are uneven, and there will be parts of medieval Europe, for example Scandinavia, or the Balkan region, that specialists on those regions will find under-represented in what follows. By contrast, the history of late medieval England has featured as the starting point of much work on medieval gender – this book points to that rich field, but does not take it as representative of the scholarship as a whole (taking four centuries of English history to form the backbone of a book titled *Gender in Medieval Culture* (2015, see Chapter 1), for example, is fine provided that the parameters are made clear: the publishers might have added a subtitle to that particular work). Many of the approaches I shall be describing were developed by historians and others who were/are not themselves medievalists, but offer ideas that can be used to read medieval texts. So whilst I will be concentrating on source materials originating in Europe from c.500 to c.1500, some of the ideas and methods we meet will be just as exciting and stimulating applied to other sources in other countries from the same or different time frames.

But it is as well to reiterate that gender history evolved (the term is used neutrally here) out of politicized women's movements, and so to a certain extent depends upon the ability of the latter in individual countries and regions to gain a foothold within academic life. In some parts of the world, women's access to education is itself still a contested issue, let alone their aspirations to higher education and activity as teachers and researchers. This does not necessarily prevent private research and study – after all, many of the female scholars who pioneered women's history in the western world in the eighteenth and nineteenth centuries (and still earlier) operated outside the academic institutions from which they were still excluded. We shall meet some of them later in the book. But the political assumptions of gender history – that it exposes the processes by which certain groups have been, or are, disempowered by others – are still too inflammatory for some students and academics to take the risk of trying to apply them to their own regions' histories, or to try to explore them within conservative institutional contexts where hierarchies are jealously preserved. Although medieval studies has a major presence in modern Japan, for instance, it is not as well established a discipline as in the West, and the study of medieval Japanese society through a gendered perspective is still freighted with issues of challenging existing academic hierarchies. That said, it would be presumptuous to suggest that such constraints undermine the work being done: there is no justification for assuming that trends emerging in the United States and United Kingdom are necessarily the 'cutting edge' and that other regions need to aspire to copy them slavishly. Gender celebrates diversity, not pecking orders.

That is not to say that the future of medieval gender history may not look very different – the globalization of medieval history, and the internet revolution mentioned above, has encouraged many medievalists to explore well beyond the boundaries of medieval Europe, and journals such as *Gender and History*, whilst not consistently publishing medieval articles, nevertheless encourage submissions from a global community. Statistically, *Gender and History* also does rather better in terms of the proportion of articles it publishes with medieval content, on average one per issue in the last ten issues. The same journal also championed a series of articles on 'Foremothers' that enabled readers to see how challenging have been the conditions in which some pioneering female and feminist historians worked (and provides a complementary collection to Chance's catalogue, see Chapter 1). *Medieval Feminist Forum*, the journal of the Society for Medieval Feminist Scholarship, in fact pre-dated the Society's formation, originally being published as a *Newsletter*. Although not all of the articles and opinion pieces published there take a historical approach, it is now recognized as having provided an important platform for the development of a feminist historical consciousness among medievalists (and in particular early career scholars seeking affirmation and support). Moreover, the easy accessibility of web-based resources has encouraged many individuals and groups to establish online-only, open access journals that challenge the monopoly of older titles and provide a platform for early career scholars, in particular, to test out their work. The drawback to such enterprises is that some seem have relatively short lives: *Third Space: A Journal of Feminist Theory and Culture*, for example, seems to have ceased publication in 2011 after ten years.

'You say "gender", I say … ?'

Much of this output is in English, and it is worth reflecting on linguistic issues before exploring the field in more detail. How gender is described – both in day-to-day life and in scholarship – can have profound effects on perceptions of status and authority. The relevant references to works in languages other than English are listed in a separate Appendix at the back of this book. They demonstrate that there is a real linguistic hurdle to negotiate in translating the English-language word 'gender' into some other languages, and thus even within Europe work might still be done under a 'women's history' banner instead. In German *Geschlecht* expresses grammatical gender, and has been adopted as a term for gender studies, but can also be used to translate 'species' or 'family', and thus is often found coupled with *Frauensgeschichte*, 'women's history'. In French *genre* has become established as the preferred term used for gender but again has a broader sense of 'type', and is used in English with that sense by literary scholars to describe textual forms. The Italian *genere* and Spanish *género* have become established terms, but only very recently. Writing in 2004, Giovanna Casagrande still placed *storia di genere* in inverted commas and added the English translation *gender history* to make clear what she was referring to. The Dumbarton Oaks online guide to bibliography on women and gender in Byzantine studies contains mainly works in English, French and German, but the complexities of expressing 'gender' in the Greek language are summed up in it having two words – *genos* for grammatical gender and *fylo* for social gender. In a relatively recent book of essays (2013, see Appendix) exploring the history of gender studies in Iberian scholarship, many of the authors have still preferred to discuss 'women *and* gender' (my emphasis).

This is reflective too of the differing rhythms of scholarship on medieval gender: for some Spanish scholars, the core issue of gender relations remains the tension between creating a separate space for women's studies and attempting to achieve equality of status by their inclusion in mainstream history syllabuses. The contributors to that volume still feel the need to assert the place of gender, rather than being sure that its place is secure. That this was still the case in 2013 might shake Anglophone scholars from a comfortable assumption that their own relative freedom to study gender, and be supported by their academic institutions and tutors in doing so, is typical or assured. Mathilde van Dijk highlights this regional difference in her consideration of why Dutch and German scholarship was also slower to embrace gender than the United States or United Kingdom, and wonders if it is simply a case of more female academics in the latter. Yet as we have already noted, gender history does not necessarily have to be practised only by female historians. Furthermore, the fact that 'gender' has now been turned into a verb in English, encouraging the 'gendering' of medieval history, complicates matters still further. A really good discussion of the difficulties of translation is contained in a French-language work, whose title translates as *Is a history without men possible?* The question it poses (and it should be noted that it was a companion volume to an earlier one that asked the same question regarding women) was essentially an entry point into gender, as opposed to women's, history.

Geographical Variations: Whose Medieval?

The global diversity of gender history is equally true of historical periodization. What is meant by the term 'medieval'? Whilst most students may have a sense of when the medieval period began and ended (conventionally, in a European framework, c.500 and c.1500CE), few students will have really considered *why* the Middle Ages are 'the bit in the middle' between the ancient and 'modern' worlds. In fact 'medieval' is essentially a Eurocentric **construct** invented by Renaissance scholars and adopted with enthusiasm by later **antiquarians** to designate – and denigrate – a period of apparent intellectual stagnancy between the glories of the Classical world and their own rediscovery of Greek and Roman philosophical, literary and scientific texts in the fifteenth and sixteenth centuries CE. The celebration of the Classical era became embedded in the educational systems of Europe, which of course were oriented entirely towards the education *of* males, *by* males, preparing them for a life of political activity and public service from which women were very much excluded. As the 'middle bit', the Middle Ages were not really credited with any great intellectual achievements.

Of course the fact that the very universities in which such ideas were being taught were themselves medieval in origin was a bit of a problem here, and it was largely dealt with by pointing to the sharp increase in foundations in the fifteenth century. Brave souls might argue that the intellectual activities of Carolingian (ninth century) or twelfth century Europe themselves constituted 'renaissances', and point out that the universities of Bologna, Oxford, Salamanca and Naples were precociously on the scene by 1300. It was equally possible to argue that universities only *really* flourished as part of *The* Renaissance. Thus a product of educated male, elitist thought became enshrined in the periodization of history. And since very few women were permitted to participate in further or higher education in the western world until the nineteenth century (and still face barriers to this day in parts of the world), few questioned this periodization, which is still retained in the academy today, despite its obvious problems when viewed from a gendered perspective. It is clear that periodization intersects with power relations and self-identity, so how does it work outside Europe?

'Medieval' in fact looks very different depending on where you are studying and what you are taught: far fewer US universities, for example, have courses on early medieval Europe (i.e. before c.1000CE) than on the later era, partly because the **nationalist** focus identified in Chapter 1, that drove nineteenth century editions of sources documenting the 'origins' of nations such as France and Germany as well as England, Italy, Spain and Portugal, has much less resonance outside Europe. For constitutional historians in the United States, early experiments in forms of republicanism, such as are visible in Italy in the twelfth and thirteenth centuries, were of much more interest, and it is the central or 'high' (c.1000–1300CE) and late (c.1300–c.1500CE) Middle Ages that claim most attention, along with a strong emphasis on the literature and culture of Europe in this era (predominantly in English studies, as already noted). (We could note in passing that Italian periodization simply distinguishes between 'alto' and 'basso' – high and low Middle Ages, with the dividing line at 1000. Note the mismatch between this and the Anglophone version.)

There has also been considerable debate, particularly since the late 1990s, about how 'medieval' works when it is applied to the same chronological period – 500 to 1500 – *outside* western Europe. Journals such as *The Medieval History Journal*, edited from and published in India since 1998, *The Medieval Globe*, a US-based enterprise (started in 2014) that nevertheless explicitly asks what global medieval history would look like, and the even newer (2015) *Medieval Worlds* journal, edited and published out of Austria, have encouraged their authors to reflect critically on the applicability of a 'Middle Ages' to other regions of the world, and have thus featured articles on Indian, Iranian, North African and other histories, to cite just some examples. The first title of the three reflects on its website that it was founded 'when the world of history was in a ferment, radically seeking a redefinition of the discipline'. The journal began with an issue situating the medieval in global culture, and was quick to include articles on gender (which was indeed still part of that perceived 'ferment' in 1998), among which were several that continued the focus on non-European texts and cultures. *The Medieval Globe* (*TMG*), and *Medieval Worlds*, by contrast, appear far more 'curated' by their editors, with thematic issues addressing large-scale questions that appear to be placing the medieval in dialogue with the concerns of later periods: health, law, empire, art. Their foundation within a year of each other may explain this similarity of approach, and the need to recognize that comparison can take place across time as well as space. The latter on its website, for instance, asks its contributors and readers to take 'a global approach to studying history in a comparative setting', and envisages also that the traditional date range might be 'extended whenever thematically fruitful if appropriate'. Significantly, although *TMG* envisages a lengthy array of future thematic issues that explore categories such as race and racializing technologies, gender finds no place on this aspirational list. Arguably, the close editorial planning that the journal reveals may reinforce, rather than challenge, existing **paradigms**.

Returning to the global and geographic middle ages, in American history, pre-1500 has traditionally been described in shorthand as 'pre-Columbian' – itself another politically charged, Eurocentric label (referring, for those unfamiliar with the term, to the time before European exploration and exploitation of the Americas, and named for the Genoese explorer Christopher Columbus, who died in 1506). In Australia, meanwhile, the debate about medieval history's value has recently been intensified by curriculum reform in schools, and again raises the important question of how 'relevant' medieval examples can be in a modern Pacific nation whose indigenous history extends back for centuries before the European 'invasion' of 1788. For scholars of India, the label 'medieval' has been adopted to describe the period of Muslim conquest and domination of much of the northern half of the peninsula (twelfth to sixteenth centuries), and in some more nationalist histories is thus a pejorative term, an interruption between the glories of ancient Hindu culture and its political re-assertion, and a swipe at Muslim Pakistan to boot. Timothy Reuter elegantly dissected the problem of comparing the 'Middle Ages' of different regions and historical traditions in an article for the first issue of *The Medieval History Journal* itself. The French scholar Marc Bloch had earlier developed a model of '**feudal** society' to assist in understanding the power dynamics of the European Middle Ages, but suggested that some or all of the elements he listed could equally well apply to Japan in the age of the *shoguns* (so 'medieval' here, by implication, would extend to 1867). Staying in the Far East, Chinese history does not readily lend itself to a 'Middle Ages' at all, although the date parameters of the journal *Early Medieval China* (Han to Tang dynasties) fall rather earlier than the equivalently named period in the West, and the imperial period extends right up to 1912, the beginning of 'modern', republican China.

This list of national 'medievals' could go on, but there is another, intersecting dynamic if we instead switch focus to religious practices, and from the dominant Christian voice to Jewish and Muslim perspectives. The Christian 'conversion era' that often opens up discussions of the European Middle Ages in the fifth and sixth centuries CE seems a rather irrelevant starting point when viewed from eastern Europe or the

Scandinavian countries, where Christianization happened rather later and/or drew upon eastern, rather than western missions. And the term has no meaning at all for the histories of Jews and Muslims. For Jewish historians, for example, the political emancipation of Jews in Europe and America in the nineteenth century represented the birth of modernity following an exceptionally long 'medieval' period, before the horrors of the Holocaust in the twentieth century ushered in significant doubts about the positive effects of modernity. And the birth of Islam of course gives rise to an entirely new dating system in Muslim sources – Muhammed's flight from Mecca in 622CE is reckoned as the start point, and years are counted from that Hijra/Hegira (so 2017 is AH 1438/9). At a stroke the idea of 'medieval' is rendered slippery, **contingent**, and frankly untenable in a global context.

Finally, 'medieval' continues to have a currency in modern media as a concise, and often totally inappropriate, way to describe events or phenomena that fall outside of modern, developed societies' ideas of civilized (another loaded term) behaviour or norms. Significantly for our purposes, the treatment of women and LGBTQ communities, and/or acts of extreme violence against them, is used as a measure of how 'medieval' and backward a particular society is. In this second decade of the twenty-first century, much of this rhetoric centres on how the modern nation state is somehow 'let down' by, or a veneer for, prevailing medieval religious and social practices, despite the fact that many of the most repressive laws are in fact relics of modern, European colonial rule. So when we are talking about '*the* Middle Ages', we need always to keep in mind the question '*whose* Middle Ages?'

Gender and Periodization

This question underpinned early feminist work challenging traditional periodization. Joan Kelly-Gadol's profoundly influential article 'Did women have a Renaissance?', first published in 1977, problematized this issue, and found its echo (at the earlier 'end' of the Middle Ages) in a study by Julia Smith critiquing a major project, sponsored by the European Science Foundation over five years between 1993 and 1998, on the

'Transformation of the Roman World'. Both these studies were preceded by a path-breaking article by feminist medieval historians Jo Ann McNamara and Suzanne Wemple, who in 1973 explored the power of early medieval women through their family connections. Originally published in *Feminist Studies*, the piece gained a wider audience when it was reprinted with amendments in a volume entitled *Women and Power in the Middle Ages* in 1988. Broadly, the article proposed a shift between informal, family-centred politics in Europe in which women could be influential, and the later institutionalization of power that excluded women on the grounds of their sex. McNamara suggested that the period before 1000 offered more space for elite women (particularly in Francia, her area of expertise) to be influential through their personal relations and kin networks, and that these opportunities narrowed after 1000, once institutional frameworks of power expressed through office-holding and state administration that bypassed such informal networks of female influence. In 2003 she published an essay in the follow-up volume to *Gendering the Master Narrative, Women and Power*, in which she developed her own and others' view of change over time to propose that the history of women, family and gender relations in fact should have the effect of 'dissolving' the Middle Ages altogether, in favour of a 'simple division between the first and second millennia'. Later work has nuanced McNamara's thesis somewhat. A new generation of scholars is investigating the power of women post-1000 and finding it not as 'exceptional' as McNamara would have had us believe (a special issue of *Medieval Feminist Forum* in 2015 published a selection of essays on this, see Chapter 1). Iberia (studied by Miriam Shadis and Ellie Woodacre), Byzantium (Barbara Hill's work), even France (Amy Livingstone's careful reconstructions) reveal evidence of elite women *still* managing estates and holding high office. We shall return to these elite women later on.

Whilst McNamara and Wemple focused on women's power, Kelly-Gadol and Smith were more concerned with the assumption of unproblematic periodization in academic practice. Both scholars criticized the failure of their academic colleagues to include considerations of gender in their analyses of major structural and cultural changes in Europe. For Kelly-Gadol, the Renaissance, far from opening up a new and exciting set of opportunities based on scientific and intellectual discoveries, in fact introduced a more oppressive framework of legal restraints on women, ever more misogynist texts on their innate weaknesses, and a more tightly enforced exclusion of women from positions of power and authority, justified by their lack of 'rational' thought (so effectively developing a continuum with McNamara and Wemple's repressive later middle ages). It is worth adding, as Kelly-Gadol did not, that if the Renaissance passed women by or had only negative effects, it was also an elite phenomenon that made little significant difference to the vast majority of the population of Europe either.

For Smith, on the other hand, the problem was even more basic: the structural, state-centred approach of the 'Transformation of the Roman World' project had privileged certain types of history, and ignored or made broad assumptions about how women fitted into models based around ethnicity, economic shifts and changes in patterns of habitation, without considering how such major developments might look different if gender was part of the equation. Moreover, focusing on the Roman world automatically positioned regions of Europe that had *not* formed part of that world as marginal to the concerns of the project.

The point to emphasize, however, is that all of these historians were using a **gendered lens** to critique the dominance of a periodization that was, and to some extent still is, shaped by a male-dominated academy, and centred on the concerns of institutional history. That McNamara's thesis of a great divide at 1000 did not stand up to more detailed scrutiny does not detract from her attempt to open up the question. Yet whilst introductory texts about the Middle Ages may now include discussions of gender, they still rarely use a gendered lens to *question* the historical period they introduce.

Taking the Long View

This chapter, however, is equally concerned with the other half of the equation: if medieval historians are at least beginning to acknowledge and challenge their (or their colleagues') gender-blindness, historians of gender relations have been rather less inclined to extend their investigations back to the **premodern**. As outlined in the introduction, the present centred political concerns of women's and gender history, when they have paid attention to the medieval era, have done so in order to compare modern conditions, favourably or not, to those of the Middle Ages. Much of the history of women's political, social and sexual emancipation, after all, is presented as one of 'progress' from a darker age of oppression, often based on views of the later Middle Ages. But taking the long view – the *longue durée* proposed by Marc Bloch and his collaborator in *Annales*, Lucien Febvre – significantly enriches modern perspectives, and highlights points of continuity as well as change. Because medieval history features far less frequently in historical training programmes than the modern era, it is up to medieval historians to lead the project to break down the period-specific barriers to dialogue. For many modern historians (and a few medievalists too, it should be added), the Middle Ages are just *too* different. This may explain why medieval historians collaborate in projects such as *Why the Middle Ages Matter*, a collection of essays that reiterates the value of thinking through modern issues of political and social justice using approaches from a different era. Such projects open up dialogues about how some neglected aspects of medieval knowledge or social practice, such as medicinal recipes, or the treatment of offenders, still have value *beyond* their historical interest. The book unfortunately passed up the opportunity to think about gender equality (or issues such as marital violence, or denial of educational opportunities) as an ongoing problem, perhaps because neither the medieval period nor the modern have really solved these problems, but there have been numerous studies that have engaged with the 'great divide' between the medieval and modern.

For example, Judith Bennett has been vocal in her argument that women's oppression forms a 'patriarchal continuum' that requires study across traditional period barriers. Using the rich resources of late medieval English records, which are sufficiently dense to enable some statistical work, Bennett herself has demonstrated the long and deep roots of the undervaluing of women's work, paid and unpaid, as another aspect of the patriarchal matrix. She has also turned her attention towards exploring the hidden lives of long-term single women, whose unmarried state marked them as different in medieval society (as it still does, to a lesser extent, today). The uncontrolled woman, choosing to live her 'lesbian-like' life alone or in the company of other women, represented a challenge to the heterosexual, marriage-centred norms of medieval *and* modern society. And – as Virginia Woolf articulated so elegantly in 1929 – having 'a room of one's own' was and is a still struggle. To these examples of social injustice we could add many more, and medieval historical research can strengthen and deepen movements of resistance.

Campaigners for women's rights in the 1970s and 1980s also focused on the dynamics of how power and knowledge were transferred between generations. Some female writers were held up as early champions of 'feminism' for pushing back against the misogynist ideas of their age, but attention also focused on women's **agency**, their ability to grasp and hold onto power and influence through their actions or life cycle events such as marriage and motherhood. A focus on women and power emerged in feminist medieval history, and was championed by scholars such as Pauline Stafford, Janet Nelson (see Chapters 4 and 5), Suzanne Fonay Wemple and others. It may be no accident in Anglophone scholarship that considerable work was done on women and power during the decade following an era of powerful women leaders of the United Kingdom, India, Pakistan and Israel (whether this will be repeated in our own era, with women leading many more nation states, is yet to be seen). Rapidly, however, the focus changed to an emphasis on women's power *in relation to* that of men, and the emergence of gender studies that explicitly offered a broader interpretation of power and emphasized its **contingency**. But whilst Joan Scott championed gender as a 'useful category of analysis', its very openness to interpretation provoked antipathy as well, as we shall see.

A gendered reshaping of the medieval starts in Chapter 3 with recognizing the gendered understanding of the human body, and the ways in which authority is claimed over it. Monica Green has been at the forefront of examining women's experiences of healthcare across a lengthy continuum, in particular the ways in which areas of medicine specific to women's bodies, gynaecology and obstetrics (the field concerned with pregnancy and childbirth) became dominated by male medical practitioners and increasingly 'medicalized' between the medieval and early modern periods. Her work engages directly with the ways in which the life and health of the baby (representing the father's living legacy) can often take precedence, still, over that of the mother, leading to invasive interventions in the birth by 'professionals'. Men's bodies, whilst not so prominent in a medical literature promoting fertility, feature more heavily in legal sources about interpersonal violence and injury, and the 'maimed man' might occupy a liminal place in his community. Also discussed is one of the most controversial (and thus stimulating) books published at the start of the 1980s, John Boswell's *Christianity, Social Tolerance and Homosexuality: Gay People in Western Europe from the Beginning of the Christian Era to the 14th Century*. Boswell's work arguably kick-started sustained research on sexuality in the Middle Ages, and opened up a space for readings of medieval texts that did not adhere to the 'norms' prescribed by many of them, but his subsequent work also implicitly challenged modern-day prejudices against same-sex relations that, far from diminishing, worsened in the 1980s as the AIDS panic took hold in the West. The responses and reactions to Boswell's work are still worth exploring in light of contemporary debates about the admissibility of same-sex marriage ceremonies, which have polarized opinion. Boswell's own 1994 book focusing on the issue, in which he identified medieval texts for such services in both the eastern and western medieval churches, takes on a new life and meaning in this context. (Boswell himself, as we shall see, was cautious about applying past situations to present concerns, but his very act of publication was a political stance.)

Modern campaigns about women's right to officiate in the Christian church have also drawn on ancient and medieval evidence for women's roles in the early Church to pursue their claims. Whilst some campaigners, such as Rosemary Radford Ruether, focused on highlighting the injustices of early religious texts, others instead sought and found precedents for female authority. Susan Ashbrook Harvey's many essays on women in the early Syriac church, and Caroline Walker Bynum's ground-breaking essays on spirituality in late medieval Europe, published in the 1980s, highlighted both the diversity of the early church, particularly in the East, and how abbots and Jesus were accorded 'maternal' roles, challenging set notions of gendered authority. The chronological gulf between these two studies has recently been partly filled by Lynda Coon's study of the fluid depictions of Jesus in manuscripts produced in the early ninth century. We shall return to women's right to claim authority to preach and teach when we look at women writers in Chapter 5. Whilst some modern congregations have now accepted the existence of female priests and bishops, the Catholic Church, literally the most medieval of institutions, remains obdurately opposed to the idea.

Hannah Skoda's recent work has sought to expose the continuing themes of domestic and other violence against women, perpetrated by men and often asserting masculinity not over the woman herself, but publicly, to other males. Domestic violence, in particular, was long seen as a private matter: the 'disciplining' of unruly wives and children was a right that the husband/father was trusted to exercise within reasonable limits. Because the Middle Ages have been depicted in both academic studies and modern media representations as endemically violent, the violence against women visible in many narratives is taken as something of a norm. In fact medieval rulers, and authors, condemned excessive violence much as the modern state does, but neither seems to have been able to resolve the issue of a significant minority of men who saw and see the beating and killing of women as intrinsic to their masculine self-image. We shall return to ways of emphasizing manhood when we explore identities in Chapter 6.

Such works, with their large chronological frames, have not been without their critics. Indeed, any attempt to argue for, and make sense of, cross-period continuities is fraught with challenges, not least the accusation of seeing anachronistic similarities across periods and the still more damning accusation that the person making the argument has no 'expertise' in the periods s/he is drawing analogies with. Bennett engaged in a sharp exchange with her critics over her boundary-crossing work. My own work on parallels between medieval and modern violence against women has had an ambivalent reception. Thinking across periods, and drawing comparisons, is *hard*, and threatening to long-held assumptions. As legal historian and medievalist William Ian Miller remarks, echoing Bennett, historians are also much more comfortable with the idea of historical change, rather than tracing continuities. Yet presenting history as a self-congratulatory, canonical story of dynamic, linear progress that excludes considerations of the ways in which subordinate groups have seen *no* change in their status, or even a worsening of their position (as mass consumerism forces ever more workers into exploitative contracts, for instance), cannot be a sustainable practice. The arbitrary, Eurocentric periodization within which medieval historians work is determined by a continued conviction that an orderly, centralized state with ambitions to expand its borders, led by a male ruler able to pursue that expansion or provide effective defence, represents the pinnacle of medieval achievements, a view bolstered by clerical texts that had a stake in this so-called strength and stability. The illusory 'achievement' of such narratives is undermined not only by a gendered view that exposes its irrelevance for the histories of women and many other subaltern groups, but also by the writing practices of medieval chroniclers, whose own works were usually shaped by religious concerns, and whose own time frames were often far longer than our own.

Medieval Sources: Chronicles and Annals

Medieval political life, broadly defined, was mapped and presented by numerous **annals** and **chronicles**, driven initially by a variety of needs. Initially, the advance of the Christian church across Europe demanded that feasts be observed correctly and on the appropriate day/s, in particular the central feast of Easter, celebrating the resurrection of Christ. The history of the Church itself formed the subject of several works, commemorating early martyrs and recording and celebrating subsequent conversions and ecclesiastical organization. Bede's history of the English church is a case in point. Such works, whilst often focusing on male clerics, also highlight the crucial role of women as supporters of, and authority figures within, the early church. Later, the writing of chronicles was often driven by the needs of rulers (or their subjects) to make sense of political changes and/or establish a convincing back-story for the existence of their **polity**. Strikingly, several of the chronicles produced in early medieval Europe start their histories not only with sections drawn from church history, but also semi-mythological origin stories of their own peoples, often centred around a prominent mother figure. A good example is Paul the Deacon's *History of the Lombards*, written at the end of the eighth century. Patrick Geary has explored some of these 'women at the beginning', and suggests that their presence at the start of some national histories enables the authors to work through 'their ambivalences about women in their own worlds'. After all, many of the examples die horrible deaths at the hands of men so that order can be restored. And of course for most of our authors biblical images abounded of women out of control. Chronicles are never neutral documents: they reflect the concerns of their writers, their writers' patrons and the prevailing societal norms (religious and cultural) that shape the understanding and explaining of the world. They are a good place to start our journey exploring the medieval period.

Source Hunt: Beginnings and Ends

For this source hunt, explore the beginnings of as many chronicles as you can, and see what was 'at the beginning'. And where are the women, and what are they doing?

Sources (and see Chapter 1)

The Anglo-Saxon Chronicle (multiple versions available in modern English translation).

Bede, *Ecclesiastical History of the English Nation*, online at http://legacy.fordham.edu/halsall/basis/bede-book1.asp.

Chronicles of the Picts, Chronicles of the Scots and other early Memorials of Scottish History, ed. W. F. Skene (Edinburgh: Constable, 1867).

Gregory of Tours, *History of the Franks*, tr. L. Thorpe (London, 1974).

Jordanes, *Origins and Deeds of the Goths*, tr. C. C. Microw (Princeton, 1915), online at https://archive.org/stream/gothichistoryof00jorduoft/gothichistoryof00jorduoft_djvu.txt.

Paul the Deacon, *History of the Lombards*, tr. W. D. Foulke (Philadelphia, 1907, repr. with an introduction by Edward Peters, 1974).

The Annals of Flodoard of Rheims, 919–966, ed. and tr. S. Fanning and B. S. Bachrach (Toronto: University of Toronto Press, 2011).

Key Reading

J. Bennett, 'Women's history: a study in continuity and change', *Women's History Review*, 2.2 (1993), 173–184.

J. Bennett, 'Theoretical issues: confronting continuity', *Journal of Women's History*, 9 (1997), 73–94.

G. Hershatter and W. Zheng, 'Chinese history: a useful category of gender analysis', *American Historical Review*, 113 (2008), 1404–1421.

J. Kelly-Gadol, 'Did women have a Renaissance?' in her *Women, History and Theory* (Chicago, IL: University of Chicago Press, 1984) [essay first published in 1977].

J. A. McNamara and S. F. Wemple, 'The power of women through the family in medieval Europe: 500–1100', *Feminist Studies*, 1.3–4 (1973), 126–141. Reprinted in *Women and Power in the Middle Ages*, ed. M. C. Erler and M. Kowaleski (Athens, GA: University of Georgia Press, 1988).

J. A. McNamara, 'Women and power through the family revisited', in *Gendering the Master Narrative: Women and Power in the Middle Ages*, ed. M. C. Erler and M. Kowaleski (Ithaca, NY and London: Cornell University Press, 2003), 17–30.

J. M. H. Smith, 'Did women have a transformation of the Roman world?' *Gender and History*, 12 (2000), 552–571.

Further Reading

J. Bennett, 'Who's afraid of the distant past?', in her *History Matters: Patriarchy and the Challenge of Feminism* (Philadelphia, PA: University of Pennsylvania Press, 2006).

Peter Burke, *The French Historical Revolution: the* Annales *School 1929–1989* (Cambridge: Polity Press, 1990).

C. Walker Bynum, *Jesus as Mother: Studies in the Spirituality of the High Middle Ages* (Berkeley, CA: University of California Press, 1984).

L. Coon, 'Gendering dark age Jesus', *Gender and History*, 28 (2016), 8–33.

Gender and Change: Agency, Chronology and Periodisation, ed. A. Shepard and G. Walker (Oxford: Blackwell, 2008).

N. Z. Davies, '"Women's history" in transition: the European case', *Feminist Studies*, 3–4 (1976), 83–103.

Editors' Introduction, *Gender and History*, 1 (1989), 1–6.

P. Geary, *Women at the Beginning: Origin Myths from the Amazons to the Virgin Mary* (Princeton, NJ: Princeton University Press, 2006).

Gender and History: Retrospect and Prospect, ed. L. Davidoff, K. McLelland and E. Varikas (Oxford: Blackwell, 1999).

M. Green, *Making Women's Medicine Masculine: The Rise of Male Authority in pre-Modern Gynaecology* (Oxford: Oxford University Press, 2008).

B. Hill, *Imperial Women in Byzantium, 1025–1204: Power, Patronage and Ideology* (London: Longman, 1999).

A. Livingstone, *Out of Love for my Kin: Aristocratic Family Life in the Lands of the Loire* (Ithaca, NY: Cornell UP, 2010).

Making Women's Histories: Beyond National Perspectives, ed. P. S. Nadell and K. Haulman (New York: New York UP, 2013).

L. Mirrer, 'Feminist approaches to medieval Spanish history and literature', *Medieval Feminist Newsletter*, 7 (1989), 3–7.

S. Mosher Stuard, 'American feminism and the *Annales* School', *Signs*, 6 (1981), 135–143.

D. Rangachari, *Invisible Women, Visible Histories: Gender, Society and Polity in North India, 7th-12th Century AD* (New Delhi: Manohar Publishers, 2009).

Religion and Sexism: Woman in the Jewish and Christian Traditions, ed. R. Radford Ruether (New York: Simon and Schuster, 1974).

K. J. Rennie, 'Introducing the Middle Ages to Australia', *History Workshop Journal*, 78.1 (2014), 265–274.

T. Reuter, 'Medieval – another tyrannous construct?' *The Medieval History Journal*, 1 (1998), 25–45.

Roman Catholic Women Priests: www.romancatholicwomenpriests.org, accessed 23 March 2015.

Joan Scott, 'Gender: a useful category of historical analysis', *AHR*, 91 (1986), 1053–1075.

M. Shadis, *Berenguela of Castile (1180–1246) and Political Women in the High Middle Ages* (New York: Palgrave, 2009).

P. Skinner, 'Viewpoint: confronting the "medieval" in medieval history: the Jewish example', *Past and Present*, 181 (2003), 219–247.

P. Skinner, 'The gendered nose and its lack: "medieval" nose-cutting and its modern manifestations', *Journal of Women's History*, 26 (2014), 45–67, and responses from Susan Mosher Stuard, 'Thinking about context', *ibid.*, 68–73; Bonnie Effros, 'Blame it on the barbarians', *ibid.*, 74–80 and Lora Wildenthal, 'The perception of suffering', *ibid.*, 81–84; and response 'The constancy of cruelty and power', *ibid.*, 85–88.

H. Skoda, *Medieval Violence: Physical Brutality in Northern France, 1270–1330* (Oxford: Oxford University Press, 2013).

P. Stafford, *Gender, Family and the Legitimation of Power: England from the Ninth to the Early Twelfth Century* (Aldershot: Ashgate, 2006).

Why the Middle Ages Matter: Medieval Light on Modern Injustice, ed. C. Chazelle, S. Doubleday, F. Lifshitz and A. Remensnyder (London and New York: Routledge, 2012).

E. Woodacre, '"Most excellent and serene lady": representations of female authority in the documents, seals and coinage of the reigning queens of Navarre (1274–1512)', in *The Image and Perception of Monarchy in Medieval and Early Modern Europe*, ed. E. Woodacre and S. McGlynn (Newcastle: Cambridge Scholars Press, 2014), 84–109.

Glossary

agency	Ability to effect change for oneself or others, independently or collaboratively
annal	A basic listing of years and events, often without further comment
antiquarian	Blanket term to describe historical interest outside later, 'professional' approaches
CE	Common Era, dating according to Christian calendar and also used to structure Jewish history-writing. Islamic history uses a different scheme (AH) based on Mohammed's flight from Mecca and on a lunar, not solar, calendar. 1AH = 622CE
chronicle	Resembling annals and produced for similar reasons, but incorporating more commentary and narrative
construct	A convenient label or concept used to structure knowledge that derives its validity from its usefulness or the power of those who use it
contingent, contingency	Reliant on other factors, not fixed
feudal	Involving ties of dependence at different levels of society
gendered lens	Imagining what a subject would look like if looked at from a starting point considering gender as the most important category of analysis
nationalist	Privileging the idea of the unified nation state, often arguing for its long establishment back into history
paradigm	A model or pattern of working, often dominant
polity	A political entity, state, community, kingdom, etc.
premodern	A catch-all term for the period before c.1800CE

3

Bodies: Sex, Sexuality and Healthcare

This chapter explores the problem of how the categories of sex and gender have been understood to correlate with nature and culture. Biological 'sex' was initially thought to be 'natural', but gender relations were a product of different actions and assumptions that were learned rather than innate. Biological sex, too, was held to be fixed, a stable category to set alongside the more fluid and changeable gender identity (or identities) that a person might embrace during their lifetime. More recent scholarship suggests that even this is not a given: what a person *looks* like physically and physiologically may not actually represent what they *feel* like: intersex persons are now recognized in medical literature as existing biologically, rather than being categorized as mentally ill and/or being forced to undergo assignation to a specific gender. The issue of the possibilities of gender *identity* in the Middle Ages will be explored in Chapter 6, below. Here we focus on the physiological world of fleshly bodies and their associated activities, and how historians have approached the question of gender in relation to the body and sexuality. Questions that they have considered include:

- how medieval authors understood the workings of the human body, in particular in relation to the central concern of reproduction;
- how bodily changes through the life course shaped gendered expectations;
- how bodies were cared for, and by whom;
- how and when bodily differences were perceived, and what meanings were assigned to this difference.

Much of the literature dealing with historical cases falls under the generic heading of 'medical history' – this is not an obvious starting point for most gender historians (and modern clinical practice itself is still grappling with how to avoid assumptions driven by ideas of gender rather than physiological difference), but in fact how bodies worked (or not) provided much of the rationale for medieval attempts to regulate, constrict and assign specific gender roles.

Bodily Histories

Ideas about women's and men's bodies in the medieval period emanated both from religious texts (Adam was created first in the Bible, Eve only as his 'helpmate') and from ancient philosophy, which privileged the male over the female as the most 'rational' being. In 1987 a foundational work was published that drew on both of these frames. Caroline Walker Bynum's *Holy Feast and Holy Fast* is a complex and often challenging read which studies the centrality of food imagery to the different modes of religious expression and devotion open to men and women in late medieval Europe (from around 1200CE). The heightened importance of **Eucharistic** devotion in this period – with Christ's body central to the act of Holy Communion – offered a space for women to make their own bodily sacrifice through prayer, contemplation and extreme fasting. Moreover, Bynum argued, because Christ was considered by medieval theology to have drawn his humanity and fleshly existence from his *mother*, and because ancient philosophy associating women's bodies with 'matter' chimed with the Old Testament imagery of Eve made from Adam's flesh, medieval women mystics were able to draw authority from their own fleshliness, that is, women's perceived weakness was actually their strength when it came to communing with the Saviour.

Bynum's work forged a bold path through complex material, including **iconography** alongside written texts, and demonstrated just how complicated the categories of 'male' and 'female' might become when seen in this particular context of religious practices. *Holy Feast* is in fact the only medieval history text to make it into Laura Lee Downs' much broader survey of gender history writing, where it is credited with making the body a central, and imperative, theme of study, 'prefigur[ing] some of the central concerns that the gendered history of the body would take up in the 1990s'. It is thus undoubtedly a landmark book, and continues to figure on gender history syllabuses to this day, but it is nevertheless a specialist text whose contents may seem impenetrable to non-specialist readers. It is also study of a particular phenomenon at a particular moment in the later Middle Ages, and thus cannot be taken as representative of how medieval people understood their bodies more generally. Bynum was not without her critics, a fact that Downs rather overlooks, but she provided a space for further study of the intersection between sex and gender, and inspired (and indeed continues to do so) a generation of historians.

Less than a decade after publishing *Holy Feast*, Bynum herself bemoaned the fact that studies of 'the body' had become a vast field of differing approaches that was not even sure what it meant by 'body', leading to 'discussions [that] are almost completely incommensurate – and often mutually incomprehensible – across the disciplines'. Of course, her own books (including *Fragmentation and Redemption*, published in 1991) had illustrated just how many ways 'bodies' could be defined, both in physical terms of her female religious undertaking fasts to control their own flesh, and in the powerful symbolic value of the Eucharistic bread/wafer as Christ's body, which some of the same women were able to visualize as flesh as well. It is not surprising, therefore, that later authors also had multiple interpretations of *the* body in mind. A collection of essays entitled *Framing Medieval Bodies*, published in 1994 (Kay and Rubin), represented the diversity of definitions, with scholars from history, archaeology and literary studies all bringing their own understandings to their contributions.

Missing from this list of approaches was an explicitly medical one, yet Bynum's work, and many of the essays in *Framing*, relied implicitly or explicitly on how medieval writers interpreted ancient medical texts, especially how these defined male and female bodies. This gap was filled by Joan Cadden's influential 1993 book on medieval sex difference, tracing how ancient ideas were transmitted into medieval medical thought. Cadden was careful to argue that there was no singular idea governing sex and gender relations as dictated by physical traits. In the earlier Middle Ages, authors drew upon the often contradictory views of the so-called Hippocratic texts (featuring 'hysterical' women with their irrational, wandering wombs), the works of Aristotle (fourth century BCE, who rejected this formulation), or the work of the Roman physician Galen in the second century CE. The latter two authors differed on the respective importance of male and female partners for the process of reproduction, and the eventual dominance of Aristotelian thought would have far-reaching implications both for medieval understandings and modern interpreters.

Aristotle acknowledged the fact that male and female were both necessary to conception, and both contributed to produce offspring, but the mother's role in this was essentially a passive one – to receive seed that would give 'form' and life to the foetal 'matter' she provided. The relative strength of both partners' contributions affected the sex of the offspring, and the birth of healthy boys was evidence that the process had completed correctly, with the male seed dominating and shaping the female matter. But the **scholastic** medicine of the twelfth and thirteenth centuries that circulated Aristotelian thought did not create gender hierarchy: as Cadden points out, 'philosophical and medical concerns *highlighted and reinforced* gender concepts but did not call them into question' [my emphasis].

The deceptive simplicity of Aristotle's model, and its prominence in medieval texts, led Thomas Laqueur to argue in 1992 that prior to the Enlightenment of the eighteenth century, men and women had essentially been seen as representing two different points on this one-sex continuum, with the female depicted as a deficient male. Laqueur's book attracted criticism for limiting itself to a discussion of the male-female binary, when in fact the one-sex model lent itself to discussions of multiple sexes and gender identities along the continuum understood by the ancients. It allowed for considerable fluidity in what was understood as 'masculine' and 'feminine'. It meant, for instance, that writers could envisage 'manly' women, 'effeminate' men (some, but not all, **eunuchs** might fall under the latter category); there was a space for the physical **hermaphrodite**, whom Roman law had sought to classify as more or less male (in order to have a legal identity). The Byzantine Empire, where eunuchs could routinely be found occupying significant posts in the imperial hierarchy, troubled western ideas of male/female relations by presenting a body that had attributes of both sexes. Laqueur's work was also criticised by Cadden for its presentation of premodern thought as essentially unified around the one-sex model, when in fact this was not at all dominant until the twelfth century, and 'medieval views ... about male and female traits suggest evidence of other models'. Ancient and medieval texts reveal far more eclecticism in their opinions as to whether women were an imperfect version of one single sex (Aristotle), or existed as a separate sex capable of generating their own seed (Galen's view, preserved in Arabic texts such as Avicenna's *Canon*). The major contrast between Aristotle's and Galen's formulations has been somewhat overstated. Cadden suggested that early translations of Greek texts into Latin were less concerned with their theoretical content and more interested in condensation, practicality and application of their remedies. The decades since Cadden's work have seen a positive explosion of work on medieval medical culture, to the extent that the stark contrast between early and later medical knowledge and practice would not now be quite so clearly drawn.

All the ancient authorities, however, broadly agreed that bodily health depended on keeping four 'humours' in balance, reflecting balance in nature (the four elements) and properties of the body (heat or cold, moisture or dryness). This simple framework enjoyed great popularity in medieval texts. Men were thought to be hotter and drier, women cooler and wetter, so any departure from those norms was to be treated with remedies that were opposites in quality. Choleric heat or fevers would be treated with cooling substances, excess blood flow (under which heading menstrual problems were often discussed) by drying, constrictive medicines. This is best represented in diagrammatic form:

hot/yellow bile (choleric)/fire   dry/black bile (melancholic)/earth

cold/phlegm (phlegmatic)/air   wet/blood (sanguine)/water

This aim to balance the humours is evident in how specific life events were treated by medical doctors.

Sex or No Sex? The Challenges of Celibacy for Women and Men

Sarah Kay and Miri Rubin suggest that 'authority over the body was contested between physicians and priests, between the clergy and the laity, and between men and women'. That is, just about everyone had a stake in their own and others' physical bodies. Central to most medical texts was a concern for reproduction, and regular sexual activity was thought not only to increase the chances of pregnancy, but also to be conducive to a healthy humoral balance for both men and women. The *regulation* of such activity through religious and **secular** laws will be addressed in the next chapter, but the tension between this model of good health and a Christian faith that celebrated examples of virginal or celibate lives, for instance, is self-evident. Kate Cooper has termed the early Christian celebration of sexual abstinence a 'revolution' that marked Christians out from adherents of other religions.

Virginity as a category has been studied at some length by medievalists, mainly because it is quite clear that it was not simply linked to whether a person had engaged in full sexual intercourse or not. Although more frequently used to describe female religious, virginity encompassed a sexually chaste life for both sexes (regardless of their previous sexual history), but also their spiritual cleanliness. Sarah Salih has explored these 'versions of virginity' in a late medieval context, enabling historians to explore beyond physical status and instead examine how female and male saints were positioned by their biographers as not only bodily chaste, but pure of spirit as well. Less visible was any discussion of how celibate women, having given up the possibility of repeated pregnancy within married life, dealt with having regular periods. It might be suggested, returning to Bynum, that the fasting and ascetic practices of medieval nuns disrupted or even stopped the menstrual flow. Sexual abstinence among women religious was promoted in the early church as a route to 'becoming male' in Christian saints' lives and advice manuals, and maintained its capacity to elevate women religious beyond their bodily status. Ironically, as we have seen, this emphasis on *transcending* the flesh would see something of a reversal in the later Middle Ages as the cult of Christ's

humanity, born of a fleshly mother, offered a different route into expressing devotion, termed **affective** piety.

Medieval authors also recognized the physical challenges of celibacy
for men as well: the problem of monks having night emissions of semen
figured early in discussions, as Conrad Leyser and others have pointed
out. What then were men to do with their bodies if they wanted to
pursue a monastic or clerical vocation? In a volume on *Medieval Masculinities*, published in 1994 Jo Ann McNamara published a controversial
yet influential essay on the '*Herrenfrage*' or 'man-question'. McNamara's
basic thesis was that the church reform movement's emphasis on clerical
celibacy in the eleventh and twelfth centuries produced a crisis in masculinity, in that the promotion of celibacy threatened men's identities *as*
men. As the Christian church reformed its practices and established an
ever-greater hold and control over the Christian community, men were
forced to decide between a life of chastity or celibacy within the church,
or more tightly regulated **monogamy** outside it.

Was there, then, a seismic shift in what it meant to be a man in the
eleventh century? Writing in 2003, McNamara revisited her thoughts on
the *Herrenfrage* and stated, 'Today I would go even further … and claim
that one of the most significant components in the millennial revolution
was the substitution of gender for class as the basic organizing principle
in the new society.' Celibate male priests, no longer allowed to define
their potency by the insemination of women, had to do so through the
rejection of women. Although McNamara does not label it as such, her
later formulation shifts the clergy from being in crisis to assuming a position of **hegemonic** masculinity, theoretically and spiritually placing them
ahead of married men, who in turn had to reinforce their status through
the subjection of their wives and other women.

Universalizing claims such as McNamara's were hard to sustain, and
somewhat exceptional already in the early 1990s. Some traditional scholars sought to engage with her work by examining the role of clergy as
men further: Robert Swanson coined the term 'emasculinity' to suggest
that, far from being McNamara's group in crisis, or celebrating their
hyper-masculinity through self-denial, celibate clergy stepped out of the
male realm altogether. He cited as support for his argument such issues

of clerical dress and the demand that clergy adopt a position of humility in imitation of Christ expressed, for example, by riding mules or donkeys rather than horses. Both these manifestations of clerical status, along with physical practices such as shaving and tonsuring, marked clerical men very visibly: what is less apparent from such a formulation is how male clergy *felt* about their different status. The relationship of religious life to masculinity has further been investigated by Patricia Cullum and Katherine Lewis, in two volumes of essays that demonstrate not only the tensions inherent for male clergy and male saints, but also the persistent use of masculine imagery in the descriptions and experiences of women religious. In their later volume published in 2013, Cullum and Lewis state that 'Clerical masculinity was generally formed in relation to other masculinities, not in relation to women', and further dismiss the idea that male religious might form a third gender (as Swanson's 'emasculine' had exemplified in 1999).

Menstruation

Successful reproduction relied upon a woman having started her periods. Bettina Bildhauer has suggested that the ideal medieval body was one that was 'bounded' and perfect, and that blood and bleeding were at the heart of much anxiety in medieval religious and literary texts. More recent studies have reflected on the skin as an inviolable body casing whose piercing and disruption were penalized in law, particularly if blood was shed. Menstruating women, therefore, were placed at an immediate disadvantage every month, as their bodies lost that integrity and became bloody and, in most religious thought, polluting. We shall return to this point.

The average age of **menarche** for medieval women has been placed around fourteen, although considerations of nutrition and life circumstances might shift that date later. Fasting women, for instance, or indeed those under stress from lack of food or security, might have experienced irregularity or cessation of periods. For ascetic nuns, losing their period may have represented a true manifestation of self-control over their bodies and sexuality. However, the regularity of periods as a means of expelling excess matter and demonstrating fertility was a regular theme in medical texts: here, menstrual blood was a positive sign, provided it was not excessive, and just after the period was the optimal time for conceiving. Even men's spontaneous bleeding from anal piles could be seen as a beneficial purge in this light. (Men's semen was also understood to be derived from blood, but men's hotter and drier bodies were more efficient in its conversion, hence they did not need to purge excess blood in the same way – the later, anti-Semitic trope of menstruating Jewish men, therefore, was a way of categorizing them as 'not-men'). Bleeding, or phlebotomy, was regularly prescribed as a further way to control this excess.

Menstruation was also a source of extreme ambivalence. It is not difficult to find medieval authors (including, for instance, the future Pope Innocent III) expressing extremely negative views of menstrual blood that ultimately drew from ancient texts, notably Aristotle and Pliny: it could rust iron, kill crops, and cause birth defects. The gaze of a menstruating woman could make a mirror look bloody, and the myth of their menstruation represented a novel way to imply that Jewish men were not really masculine. The thirteenth century treatise known as *The Secrets of Women*, produced in Germany and falsely attributed to Albertus Magnus, adds that a menstruating woman gave off poisonous fumes that can blind babies in their cradles. Menstruation was cited as evidence of women's weakness (social anthropologist Mary Douglas explored menstruation – women's inherent leakiness – as part of her classic study on pollution and taboos, which has influenced generations of medievalists dealing with texts). All three major religions saw it as a polluting phenomenon within marriage and forbade sexual intercourse whilst a woman was bleeding. The taboo extended also to **postpartum** bleeding after the birth of children, but acknowledged that sexual relations should resume once the woman was cleansed – Elisheva Baumgarten has compared these moments of separation from the community in Christian and Jewish culture.

As Monica Green points out, it is rare to find a *medical* author referring to the alleged evils of menstrual blood, since its regular (but not excessive) flow was an essential of good health and fecundity. Menstruation was, in the medical literature, an absolutely necessary means for a woman's body to purge itself of impurities, a sign both of regular health and of her fertility. Its cessation when the woman was pregnant was thought to be a sign that blood was now being turned into mother's milk. This is why it has such a central place in medical texts: the absence of menses had implications not only for women, but their husbands and families. One problem that medical authors do address is the proper age for a girl to start sexual relations, and somewhat surprisingly this might not be straight after her first period, since girls' bodies, whilst now showing the sign of being fertile, might not yet be physically mature enough to cope with the process of giving birth. Such a common-sense view is somewhat lacking in regulatory texts, however. Medieval law codes and church canons considered the age of twelve to be a suitable minimum for girls to marry, with fourteen recommended for boys. That is not to say that such guidelines were followed: laws sometimes had to be restated to defend younger children, and the common elite habit of engaging very young children in marriage agreements, to be fulfilled when they were of age, led to a significant number of cases being heard in church courts where one or both of the partners was unwilling or unable to consummate the marriage.

Sexuality and Fecundity

A married couple might expect to have a large family, assuming both were well, fertile and able engage in sex regularly. Whether or not medieval couples co-operated in regulating their families through the use of contraceptive devices and recipes is still open to question: John Riddle was firmly of the view that women, in particular, did make use of **contraceptive** and **abortifacient** substances. He was no doubt influenced by warnings in medical texts about the ability of some plants to have such effects, and perhaps also by misogynist texts such as the *Secrets of Women* that took a default position on women's ability to deceive their husbands. In their reviews of his work, Monica Green and Helen King have both taken issue with Riddle's thesis, for different reasons, but as we shall see later in this chapter, there is ample evidence to suggest that not only theoretical texts, but medical compendia designed for use in the household, incorporated advice on menstrual regulation that, whilst thought necessary for procreation, could also be a way to provoke a purging of foetal matter.

Discussions about sex and gender in the Middle Ages have included discussions about medieval sexuality. For Ruth Mazo Karras, this means 'erotic desire' and the meanings that people attributed to sex acts, not the acts themselves. 'Sexuality', therefore, allows for a spectrum of desires but does not impose the requirement that we can account for all of them, nor impose modern categories on what can be quite evasive or intransigent materials. What is clear from Karras's discussion, however, is that sexual relations between men and women were understood to be a transitive act between an active, dominant male and a passive, receptive female. The pleasure to be had from sex was, in Christian and Jewish texts at least, secondary to the purpose of procreation (and led to rabbinical anxieties about the pleasure Jewish women might get if they lay with uncircumcized men). Yet in Islamic medical traditions, female pleasure in the sex act was part and parcel of the successful generation of children. Rich comparative work is now being done on gender and medicine in these communities in both Northern Europe (Christians and Jews) and the Mediterranean (Christians, Jews and Muslims), where different traditions coexisted between and within faith groups on matters of marriage, sexuality and childbirth.

A great deal has been written by historians eager to see an empowerment of medieval women through motherhood. The 1996 edited volume *Medieval Mothering* (Parsons and Wheeler) opened up some of the possibilities in a collection of essays notable for its wide geographical coverage. The examples discussed there and in subsequent collections, however, are mainly of elite women, and the reality of serial births for many or most women may have felt more debilitating than empowering. Indeed, Norfolk businesswoman Margery Kempe's decision to embrace a celibate life, after having visions of Christ, is eminently explicable if we remember she had by that time given birth to fourteen children (her life will be explored further in Chapter 6). Large families meant many hands for work, but many mouths to feed, and the physical effects of repeated pregnancy on women's bodies, though well-known medically today (and including iron deficiency, hip displacement, sepsis and other complications), have only recently begun to be investigated systematically by historians and archaeologists.

Complicating Categories: Singledom as a State of Being

So far we have discussed sexual activity within heterosexual marriage as a default state, and assumed that this was a near-inevitable pathway for Jewish, Muslim and Christian men and women, unless the latter chose, or were forced, to enter the Church. Even this diversion might not end sexual activity – the reforming tendencies noted above must have had something to reform, and married and cohabiting priests, errant monks and nuns, and sexually experienced men and women who decided in later life to embrace chastity, enter religious orders or live as part of a religious community, all complicate attempts to define categories. Cordelia Beattie has addressed the thorny issue of social categorization – how it operated in late medieval England, and still influences modern scholarly understandings of the Middle Ages – in order to explore the lives of single women and men. Singledom is of course as much a legal category – absence of marriage – as a bodily one: unmarried men and women could still be sexually active, and the recognition of a 'marriage' might lie simply in the act of consummation. It is telling that most work on singledom, by Beattie, Kim Phillips, Judith Bennett and Amy Froide, among others, has tended to utilize late medieval evidence, when both church and state had a clear stake in validating and regulating unions. Nevertheless, the example of singledom reminds us that **heteronormativity** is embedded within the assumptions of most medieval authors and their modern interpreters, and looking for individuals and groups who resist categorization or are portrayed as anomalous or transgressive often opens up a much more interesting spectrum of relationships, in which monogamous marriage might feature, but was certainly not the only possibility. Never-married men and women, same-sex couples, plural marriages, commercial bodily transactions (termed 'prostitution' by regulators) and intersex bodies all made up the corporal life of medieval Europe. They are only exceptional in the sense that they are less frequently documented.

Same-Sex Relationships

The assumed heteronormativity of the medieval period, however, has long had its critics. In 1980 the publication of John Boswell's *Christianity, Social Tolerance and Homosexuality: Gay People in Western Europe from the Beginning of the Christian Era to the Fourteenth Century (CSTH)* hone a light on the modern prejudices that had at best overlooked and at worst suppressed the histories of gay people in academic scholarship. Initially, the book was an exercise in re-reading ancient and Biblical texts to claim that these could not have formed the basis of such prejudices, given their clear evidence of tolerating same-sex relationships. Boswell argued strongly that re-reading these texts revealed a hidden history of same-sex (and usually male) relations, and that popular prejudice, not religious belief, often lay at the heart of intolerance. 'Religious beliefs may cloak or incorporate intolerance', he stated in 1980, 'But careful analysis can almost always differentiate between conscientious application of religious ethics and the use of religious precepts as justification for personal animosity or prejudice'. Like women's history before it, documenting **gay** history, for Boswell, was shaped by contemporary concerns of acceptance and legal rights. Unlike women's history, however, the subjects of gay history had to be actively sought out, since 'in hostile societies they become invisible' and are unable to establish a group identity in quite the same way.

What, though, did 'gay' mean? In an extensive section on 'Definitions', *CSTH* drew a distinction between the label '**homosexual**', applied to gay people and often used in a hostile manner, and 'gay', which for Boswell indicated a conscious desire to engage with others of the same-sex in a spectrum of relationships. These might not include sexual intercourse at all: his use of the term 'gay sensibilities' is helpful in identifying people in whom 'the primary focus of their love relationships was confined to their own gender'. This is an important point that gets overlooked in cursory reviews and criticism of the book: what Boswell is doing, in the subsequent pages, is simply opening up the *possibility* of alternative readings of texts or, in short, queering the view.

One of Boswell's more interesting ideas in *CSTH* was that same-sex relations particularly thrived in urban environments, to the extent that a 'gay subculture' could be posited, and that urban decline in the late Roman and early medieval periods had the effect not so much of suppressing such relations as reducing potential sources for them. **Secular** laws forbidding homosexual relationships were passed in this period, it was true, but were rarely enforced, and Boswell suggests that insofar as the Church was concerned, 'homosexual behavior [was] no more (and probably less) reprehensible than comparable heterosexual behavior (i.e. extramarital)'. Furthermore, the establishment of monastic houses and schools fostered visibly intense relationships between teachers and pupils, and clerical letters from the early Middle Ages onwards were distinctly erotic in nature. Thus for Boswell prominent medieval clerics such as Alcuin, Marbod of Rennes and St Aelred all revealed their gay sexuality in their correspondence with and poems to boys and other men. As medieval European urban culture revived, so did the gay subculture that had characterized Greece and Rome, and the eleventh and twelfth centuries, for Boswell, are a high point in the production of gay literary output, before ideas about social, religious and intellectual conformity kicked in during the thirteenth century. (Boswell's model thus anticipates Robert I. Moore's influential *Formation of a Persecuting Society* by nearly a decade, for all that Moore did not include sexuality in his analysis.)

CSTH faced criticism from reviewers for his focus on male-male relationships and for 'over-reading' the medieval evidence as incontrovertible proof of a gay subculture in the modern sense. Boswell responded to his critics in an article expanding on his methodology published in a rather obscure journal in 1983 (and reprinted six years later when LGBT history had finally begun to move into the academic mainstream). Brian McGuire published an extended rejection of Boswell's model of monastic same-sex relations in 1988, arguing that the clerical letters – which were after all hardly private documents – could at best be read as evidence of friendship, and that the love on show here was shaped by biblical models, not sexual preferences. (The horror of '**sodomy**' expressed in clerical texts, it was argued, suggests that had the letter exchanges been between male *sexual* partners, they would rapidly have lost their often high positions in the church.) Not surprisingly, therefore, Boswell took some time (and published a classic book on child abandonment) before returning to issues of sexuality in *Same-Sex Unions in Pre-Modern Europe*, published in 1994, the year of his death. In this, he adopted a rather bruised and cautious tone as he explored texts from the eastern church that could be interpreted as **liturgical** texts for gay marriage ceremonies. His awareness of the possibility of continued hostility is evident in his language: he does not name the 'correspondent' who had drawn his attention to the texts, and at the end of the book he observes that:

> It is not the province of the historian to direct the actions of future human beings, but only to reflect accurately on those of the past … Recognizing that many – probably most – earlier Western societies institutionalized some form of romantic same-sex union gives us a much more accurate view of the immense variety of human romantic relationships and social responses to them than does the prudish pretense that such "unmention-able" things never happened.

Such a defensive tone was understandable: if anything *Same-Sex Unions* attracted even more hostile criticism in both the academic and popular press. It was left to others to respond to the hostility, and the John Boswell page of the Internet Medieval Sourcebook offers the opportunity to read reviews and the responses of the site's manager, Paul Halsall, to some of the most vitriolic.

Boswell's work, for all its perceived methodological flaws, remains an important milestone in the history of gender and sexuality. Subsequent generations of scholars have revisited 'the Boswell thesis' to expand upon, and critique, the many case studies he included in *CSTH*, and a '35th Anniversary Edition' of the book was published by University of Chicago Press in 2015, acknowledging its status as a ground-breaking text. The debates it engendered are still continuing.

CSTH was very much of its time in its frustration with the scholarly silence, or ignorance, of gay people and their lives. Adrienne Rich had already published an essay in *Signs* lamenting 'compulsory heterosexuality' as an approach to studying culture and history, calling on women to act collectively to push back against this 'master narrative'. Boswell's own work inspired further work from medievalists, re-examining the sources he used, and opening up new lines of enquiry. Eve Kosofsky

Sedgwick in 1985 turned her eye to literary texts and adopted the idea of '**homosocial**' as a way of understanding the close male-male relationships on view among the protagonists of medieval romance, an idea that swiftly took hold in the work of subsequent commentators and most recently has been applied to women as well as men. Julian Haseldine's edited volume on friendship features homosociality as a concept, suggesting that Sedgwick's formulation was rather less politically charged, albeit often no less erotic. Today we might substitute the word 'bromance' to express the same idea, that men could form quite intensely close relationships without necessarily engaging in sexual activity. Tom Linkinen has taken a slightly different approach to same-sex sexuality, echoing many of Boswell's doubts about the fixity of terms such as sodomy in late medieval English culture, but suggesting that some of the hostility to same-sex relationships was due to their challenging of gender norms – for a man to take a sexually passive role was indeed 'against nature', feminizing him and undermining the purpose of sex as outlined in Chapter 4, procreation. All-female relationships, too, were similarly 'against nature' for the same reason, although less often discussed in medieval sources.

Though all-female relationships were less well documented, much rich work has been done on women's religious communities with an eye to asking whether same-sex partnerships were visible in such settings. (Boswell was far more forthcoming on this issue in his 1995 volume than in his earlier work.) It was initially assumed that women's inability to inseminate meant that their affective relationships with each other did not threaten traditional gender hierarchies, unlike adulterous unions between a man and someone else's wife, and this explains why we have so little documented evidence of how female, same-sex relationships were regarded in medieval society. Yet the few cases we do have perhaps suggest that there was hostility: in the early fifteenth century a young married woman from France, Laurence, is documented appealing for her release from prison having engaged in sexual activities with a girl named Jehanne. Was she being punished as an adulteress? On a more positive note, Judith Bennett has used the term 'lesbian-like' to describe a number of female communities or groups in medieval culture whose lives were enriched by the mentorship and companionship of other women. Importantly, focusing on the language used in affective relationships – Linkinen's final chapter on the positive possibilities of same-sex *love*, rather than *sex*, epitomizes this broadening of approach – enabled a spectrum of possible relationships to be suggested.

Corporal Malfunction: Impotence, Infertility, Impairment

In her formulation of what made a medieval man, Jo Ann McNamara placed men's sexual prowess, their ability to father children, as central to their being male. Medical and surgical texts of the period between the fifth and fifteenth centuries did not just address issues of female reproduction. Although the common view was that failure to conceive was a woman's problem, there was some acknowledgement that men shared responsibility, either in insufficient seed or inability to have and maintain an erection for intercourse. The twelfth century medical compendium known as the *Trotula* contained a remedy that tested both partners in a marriage that had failed to produce children. In a German article published in 2009, Klaus van Eickels (see Appendix) suggests that medieval noblemen who suspected they were unable to father children (through lack thereof in previous sexual and extramarital activities) were likely to accept childless marriages rather than put aside their wives and attract attention to their problem. Impotence, on the other hand, attracted attention when wives sought to end their unconsummated marriages through the church courts. Proving impotence might lead to hands-on, and well-documented, tests in court by women specifically brought in to test the man's lack of ability. The frequent association of impotence with women's magic may explain striking illustrations of male phalluses being plucked by women (and nuns) in a number of contexts, including murals (as at Massa Marittima in Italy) and manuscript decorations, with the penises often hanging from trees in a direct reference to their life-giving potential.

Successful conception and pregnancy was expected to end in healthy offspring, but this did not always happen. Legal texts speak of acts of violence resulting in women miscarrying, and a minority of children born (we have no way of quantifying the percentage) with impairments that affected their life chances. Gender's concern with the subaltern has led to a wave of work on bodily difference in the Middle Ages, leading to questions of how physical or mental **impairment** was perceived and might lead to **disability**. After all, a body that did not conform to the norm might be an object of wonder, awe or hostile suspicion – its owner excited curiosity. Many medieval authors (such as Gregory of Tours in the sixth century and Gerald of Wales in the late twelfth) take an interest in, and report, unusual births, be they of conjoined twins, babies with additional or missing limbs, or other 'defects'. Whilst the penchant for reporting these as 'monstrous' births belongs more accurately to the early modern period than the medieval, such babies did attract attention. Theorists of **monstrosity**, however, do not simply deal in the concrete – rather, they explore the latent fears of a given group about its own propensity to become monstrous. The work of Jeffrey Jerome Cohen has been influential in the burgeoning field of monster theory, proposing a series of ways in which the monster inhabits places of fear within a society – it represents what is different, external and unknown, certainly, but it also expresses what is latent *within* that society, just waiting to burst out. Thus an unusual birth might raise questions about the respective roles of mother and father. What latent qualities in the parents were expressed in their baby? Several texts of the twelfth and thirteenth centuries imagined that specific physical injuries acquired in adulthood could be transferred to offspring, and such stories were often a way of confirming questions of paternity.

Care is needed, however, in utilizing narrative sources: the Pisan annals for 1157 report the birth of a boy in Bologna with a beard, a full head of hair and teeth; the Polish annals for 1274 tell a more elaborated tale of a boy born with a full set of teeth and the power of speech, which both disappeared when he was baptized. Whilst the first report *might* represent an anomalous birth, the second clearly portrays a didactic picture of demonic intervention that is driven out by Christian baptism. Modern authors disagree, however, on how children with impairments were welcomed into medieval society. For some archaeologists, the marginalized burials of people with bodily impairments reflected their marginalization in life; for others, the distinction set in when these people reached adulthood and were unable to take up 'adult' social roles, leaving children as an undifferentiated category whether impaired or not, and perhaps even enjoying special treatment to mitigate their impairment. For historian Jacques Le Goff, illness, disease and impairment were ubiquitous in medieval society, reducing the potential for disabilities to make much difference to an individual's life. All of these issues concern the gender historian, as they represent another intersection: sex, physical incapacity and perceived economic burden (or even impaired capacity to reproduce) could all combine to affect a child's future opportunities as s/he grew up.

Bodies of Knowledge

Traditional medical history, untroubled by issues of gender, has tended to favour tracing the intellectual pursuit of medical knowledge over its practical applications, partly because the latter are so hard to document reliably. Yet many, even most, health challenges of the medieval period must have been confronted and addressed in a domestic context, and knowledge passed down through generations. Scholastic texts co-existed with more practical collections of remedies which, whilst they might still cite ancient authorities, were intended to help patients on the ground. The citations, it might be noted, were not always accurate, as editors of these collections are now discovering. Some medical texts, as Monica Green has demonstrated in the case of the ensemble collected in the twelfth and thirteenth centuries and known as the *Trotula*, were written as if by a woman in order to allow discussion of women's problems (the *Treatments for Women* within the collection, however, was indeed written by a female author, Trota of Salerno).

Medical history has also dealt unproblematically with the ways in which men's and women's bodies were cared for, and it has taken a generation of feminist scholars to point out the ways in which the development of a medical 'profession' was a means by which women's practice was gradually and deliberately devalued. Early feminist work focused on the documenting of female medical practitioners, including those working as midwives, exposing the constraints placed upon these women as medicine increasingly became a licensed and regulated profession from the thirteenth century onwards. Monica Green herself explored the colonizing and medicalization of female bodies by male practitioners in her study of medieval and early modern obstetrics, and continues to promote the study of medieval medicine in dialogue with other disciplines.

This gender-sensitive work has broadened out into a wider consideration of forms of practice that did *not* require licensing, and a substantial reappraisal of the possibilities of treatment at home, where surely the vast majority of ailments and injuries were cared for. The shift that took place from the thirteenth century onwards towards more and more texts written and compiled in vernacular languages opened a route to medical knowledge that had previously been confined to the 'literate' in Latin. Library and archival collections teem with medieval medical compendia from the thirteenth to sixteenth centuries that often mix **vernacular** recipes with astronomical and astrological observations, extracts from medical authorities, prayers and charms. Read holistically, such works, which are sometimes compiled in a small enough format to suggest they could be carried around and consulted easily, speak volumes about the medieval concern with reproductive health in particular. Not only remedies to provoke or control menstruation (which could equally be read as a means to have abortions), but also the position of stars, the moon, the religious calendar and folklore were employed to ensure a good outcome, the birth of many healthy children. Yet such texts have tended to be mined only for their recognizably 'medical' parts (identified by their similarity to existing, known medical texts), ignoring or downplaying elements that today might be considered the 'complementary medicine' or at the very least an arsenal of methods to reassure the patient and their family. This skew in the scholarship has undoubtedly led to female and non-elite agency in the world of medieval healing being overlooked.

Thanks largely to the efforts of Helen King (for antiquity), Joan Cadden, Monica Green and their students, gender has now been embedded within premodern medical history, and whilst the project to identify female practitioners continues, attention is now being paid to the ownership and readership of the vernacular compendia. The equation of vernacular texts with female readers is too simplistic – a gendered analysis in fact focuses on the power that such texts offered to men *and* women to cooperate in their own and others' care at familial and community level, as the work of Elizabeth Mellyn is demonstrating. Whilst not a true democratization of medicine – we must note how fiercely protective the new universities were of their right to license new practitioners (as Geneviève Dumas has illustrated in the case of Montpellier in France, see the Appendix) – this spreading of knowledge has not yet been sufficiently explored.

From Bodies to Ideologies

Considering the sick, imperfect body encourages historians to question how many of our assumptions about medieval Christian society – its warrior masculinity, its emphasis on reproduction as the desired outcome of sex (or chastity as a more laudable option), the 99% of people who worked the land and supported themselves and others with their labour – require reconsideration. Irina Metzler has recently raised such questions in her social history of disability in the Middle Ages, but again there is room for much more work in this area. The Middle Ages lacked modern medical science's ability to repair, reshape and rehabilitate the maimed body with robotic aids and prosthetics. Such abilities in the twenty-first century have provoked debate on whether we have now entered the age of the 'post-human' the recipients of such treatments representing a new category of being. This suggests that the damaged or different body is somehow viewed as not-human, a theme that medieval historians, ironically, have long been familiar with.

The idea of women's secondary status did not disappear once medical science had decided there were two distinct sexes (a development pre-dating the secure discovery of the X and Y chromosomes of sex determination in the early twentieth century), and thus discarded the 'women-as-deficient-male' model. In fact the assertion of difference in physiology (which medieval texts had in fact prefigured) was largely responsible for some of the ideas we are about to meet about women's confinement to a separate, domestic sphere: their brains were smaller, after all, and their bodies physiologically weaker. Instead of being defective men, bad enough, this new, separate sex could be loaded with incapacities (lack of reason, lack of physical capacity) justifying its exclusion from all kinds of activity. The results of this for legal identity and access to education and political activity were profound.

Source Hunt: Reading Bodies

How are bodies presented in medieval medical texts, and what are the central concerns of medical literature? How is sexuality represented, and what norms and exceptions are visible?

Sources

S. Allott, tr., *Alcuin of York, c. AD732–804: His Life and Letters* (York: William Sessions Limited, 1974).

W. Frölich, tr., *The Letters of St Anselm of Canterbury*, 3 vols (Kalamazoo, MI: Cistercian Publications, 1990).

Corpus of Early English Medical Writing, at the University of Helsinki, Finland: www.helsinki.fi/varieng/series/volumes/14/taavitsainen_pahta/#ceem.

Tony Hunt, *The Medieval Surgery* (Woodbridge: Boydell, 1992).

Faith Wallis, ed., *Medieval Medicine: A Reader* (Toronto, ON: University of Toronto Press, 2010).

Patricia Skinner and Elisabeth van Houts, eds, *Medieval Writings on Secular Women* (London: Penguin, 2011): organised according to life-cycle stages, thus with many excerpts dealing with reproduction.

Monica H. Green, ed., *The Trotula: A Medieval Compendium of Women's Medicine* (Philadelphia, PA: University of Pennsylvania Press, 2001).

H. Rodnite Lemay, tr., *Women's Secrets: A Translation of Pseudo-Albertus Magnus' De Secretis Mulierum with Commentaries* (New York: SUNY Press, 1992).

Key Reading

J. Bennett and A. L. Froide, eds, *Singlewomen in the European Past, 1250–1800* (Philadelphia: University of Pennsylvania Press, 1998).

J. Boswell, 'Revolutions, universals and sexual categories', *Salmagundi*, 58–59 (1982–3), 89–113; reprinted in M. Duberman, M. Vicinus and G. Chauncey, eds, *Hidden from History: Reclaiming the Gay and Lesbian Past* (New York: New American Library, 1989), 17–36.

C. Walker Bynum, *Holy Feast and Holy Fast: The Religious Significance of Food to Medieval Women* (Berkeley, CA: University of California Press, 1987).

C. Walker Bynum, 'Why all the fuss about the body? A medievalist's perspective', *Critical Inquiry*, 22 (1995), 1–33.

J. Cadden, *The Meanings of Sex Difference in the Middle Ages* (Cambridge: Cambridge University Press, 1993).

M. Green, 'Flowers, poisons and men: menstruation in medieval western Europe', in Andrew Shail and Gillian Howie, eds, *Menstruation: A Cultural History* (London/New York: Palgrave Macmillan, 2005), 51–64.

R. Mazo Karras, *Sexuality in Medieval Europe: Doing unto Others* (New York: Routledge, 2005).

J. A. McNamara, 'The *Herrenfrage*: the restructuring of the gender system 1050–1150', in C. A. Lees, ed., *Medieval Masculinities: Regarding Men in the Middle Ages* (Minneapolis, MN: Minnesota University Press, 1994), pp. 3–29.

J. A. McNamara, 'Women and power through the family revisited', in *Gendering the Master Narrative: Women and Power in the Middle Ages*, ed. M. C. Erler and M. Kowaleski (Ithaca, NY and London: Cornell University Press, 2003), 17–30.

Further Reading

E. Baumgarten, ed., *Mothers and Children: Jewish Family Life in Medieval Europe* (Princeton, NJ: Princeton University Press, 2004).

C. Beattie, *Medieval Single Women: The Politics of Social Classification in Late Medieval England* (Oxford: Oxford University Press, 2007).

J. Bennett, '"Lesbian-like" and the social history of lesbianisms', *Journal of the History of Sexuality*, 9 (2000), 1–24.

J. Boswell, *Christianity, Social Tolerance and Homosexuality: Gay People in Western Europe from the beginning of Christianity to the 14th Century* (Chicago, 1980; 35th Anniversary Edition with a new introduction by M. D. Jordan, Chicago, 2015).

J. Boswell, *Same-Sex Unions in Premodern Europe* (New York: Vintage, 1994). See also the pages on Boswell's work, including reviews and a full bibliography, on the Internet Medieval Sourcebook: https://legacy.fordham.edu/halsall/pwh/index-bos.asp.

Vern Bullough, 'On being male in the middle ages', in Clare Lees, Thelma Fenster and Jo Ann McNamara, eds, *Medieval Masculinities: Regarding Men in the Middle Ages* (Minneapolis, MN: University of Minnesota Press, 1994).

V. Bullough and J. A. Brundage, eds, *The Handbook of Medieval Sexuality* (New York: Garland, 1996).

Carmen Caballero-Navas, 'Secrets of women: naming female sexual difference in medieval Hebrew medical literature', *Nashim: A Journal of Jewish Women's Studies and Gender Issues*, 12 (2006), 39–56.

John Carmi Parsons and Bonnie Wheeler, eds, *Medieval Mothering* (New York and London; Garland, 1996).

D. Clark, *Between Medieval Men: Male Friendship and Desire in Early Medieval English Literature* (Oxford: Oxford University Press, 2009).

J. J. Cohen, 'Monster theory: seven theses', in his edited volume *Monster Theory: Reading Culture* (Minneapolis, MN: Minnesota University Press, 1996).

Kate Cooper, *The Virgin and the Bride: Idealized Womanhood in Late Antiquity* (Cambridge, MA: Harvard UP, 1999).

L. Crompton, 'The myth of lesbian impunity: capital laws from 1270–1791', *Journal of Homosexuality*, 6 (1980/1), 11–25.

P. H. Cullum and K. Lewis, eds, *Holiness and Masculinity in the Middle Ages* (Cardiff: University of Wales Press, 2004).

P. H. Cullum and K. Lewis, eds, *Religious Men and Masculine Identity in the Middle Ages* (Woodbridge: Boydell, 2013).

M. Douglas, ed., *Purity and Danger* (London: Routledge, 1966).

Laura Lee Downs, *Writing Gender History* (2nd ed., London: Bloomsbury, 2010).

Dynamis, vol. 34, issue 2: Special Issue on Childbirth and Women's Healthcare in pre-Modern Societies, including Egypt, Europe and Japan.

K. Eisenbichler and J. Murray, eds, *Desire and Discipline: Sex and Sexuality in the Premodern World* (Toronto, ON: University of Toronto Press, 1996).

J. Eyler, ed., *Disability in the Middle Ages* (New York: Ashgate, 2010).

N. Giffney, M. Sauer and D. Watt, eds, *The Lesbian Premodern* (New York: Palgrave Macmillan, 2011).

R. Gilchrist, ed., *Medieval Life: Archaeology and the Life Course* (Woodbridge: Boydell, 2012).

R. Godden and J. Hsy, 'Analytical survey: encountering disability in the middle ages', *New Medieval Literatures*, 15 (2013), 313–339.

M. Green, ed., *Making Women's Medicine Masculine* (see above, Chapter 2).

J. Haseldine, ed., *Friendship in Medieval Europe* (Stroud: Sutton, 1999).

Liz James, ed., *Women, Men and Eunuchs: Gender in Byzantium* (London and New York: Routledge, 1997).

W. Johnson, 'The myth of Jewish male menses', *Journal of Medieval History*, 24 (1998), 273–295.

Sarah Kay and Miri Rubin, eds, *Framing Medieval Bodies* (Manchester: Manchester University Press, 1994).

H. King, *Hippocrates' Women: Reading the Female Body in Ancient Greece* (London and New York: Routledge, 1998).

M. Kuefler, ed., *The Boswell Thesis: Essays on Christianity, Social Tolerance and Homosexuality* (Chicago: University of Chicago Press, 2006).

T. Laqueur, ed., *Making Sex: Body and Gender from the Greeks to Freud* (Cambridge, MA: Harvard University Press, 1992).

C. Leyser and L. Smith, eds, *Motherhood, Religion and Society in Medieval Europe, 400–1400* (Farnham and Burlington, VT: Ashgate, 2011).

T. Linkinen, *Same-Sex Sexuality in Later Medieval English Culture* (Amsterdam: AUP, 2015).

K. Lochrie, C. Schulz and P. McCracken, eds, *Constructing Medieval Sexuality* (Minneapolis, MN: Minnesota University Press, 1997).

K. Lochrie, 'Don't ask, don't tell: murderous plots and medieval secrets', *GLQ: A Journal of Lesbian and Gay Studies*, 1.4 (1995), 405–417, revised and reprinted in Louise Fradenberg and Carla Freccero, eds, *Premodern Sexualities* (New York: Psychology Press, 1996).

E. Mellyn, 'Passing on secrets: interactions between Latin and vernacular medicine in medieval Europe', *I Tatti Studies*, 16 (2013): 289–310.

I. Metzler, *Disability in Medieval Europe: Thinking about Physical Impairment during the High Middle Ages* (London/New York: Routledge, 2006).

I. Metzler, *A Social History of Disability in the Middle Ages: Cultural Considerations of Physical Impairment* (London/New York: Routledge, 2013).

R. Middlemass and T. Tyers, 'Disabling masculinity: manhood and infertility in the high middle ages', in S. Crawford and C. Lee, eds, *Social Dimensions of Medieval Disease and Disability* (Oxford: BAR Publications, 2014), 47–58.

S. Miller, *Medieval Monstrosity and the Female Body* (New York/London: Routledge, 2010).

Robert Mills and Bettina Bildhauer, eds, *The Monstrous Middle Ages* (Cardiff: University of Wales Press, 2003).

L. L. Otis, *Prostitution in Medieval Society: The History of an Urban Institution in Languedoc* (Chicago: University of Chicago Press, 1985).

N. F. Partner, 'No sex, no gender', *Speculum*, 68 (1993), 419–443.

Kim Phillips, 'Warriors, Amazons and Isles of Women: medieval travel writing and constructions of Asian femininities', in *Intersections of Gender, Religion and Ethnicity in the Middle Ages*, ed. C. Beattie and K. A. Fenton (London and New York: Palgrave Macmillan, 2011), 183–207.

I. Resnick, 'The medieval roots of the myth of Jewish male menses', *Harvard Theological Review*, 93 (2000).

A. Rich, 'Compulsory heterosexuality and lesbian existence', *Signs*, 5 (1980), 631–660.

J. Riddle, *Contraception and Abortion from the Ancient World to the Renaissance* (Cambridge, MA: Harvard University Press, 1992).

C. Rider, *Magic and Impotence in the Middle Ages* (Oxford: Oxford University Press, 2006).

S. Salih, *Versions of Virginity in Late Medieval England* (Woodbridge: Boydell, 2001).

F. Canadé Sautman and P. Sheingorn, eds, *Same-Sex Love and Desire among Women in the Middle Ages* (London: Palgrave, 2001).

D. Sayer and S. D. Dickinson, 'Reconsidering obstetric death and female fertility in Anglo-Saxon England', *World Archaeology*, 45.2 (2013), 285–297.

E. Kosofsky Sedgwick, *Between Men: English Literature and Male Homosocial Desire* (New York, Columbia University Press, 1985).

E. Kosofsky Sedgwick, *Tendencies* (Durham, NC: Duke University Press, 1993).

Social History of Medicine, vol. 29 issue 2: Special Issue on Infertility in Medieval and Early Modern Medicine.

D. Wilson, *Signs and Portents: Monstrous Births from the Middle Ages to the Enlightenment* (London and New York: Routledge, 1993).

Glossary

abortifacient	Able to provoke the body to expel a foetus
affective	Describing forms of piety and devotion that place the worshipper in direct contact with Christ, Mary or the saints
celibacy	Refraining from sexual activity
contraceptive	Preventing semen from fertilizing an egg
disability	The societal limitations placed on a person with an impairment, which might or might not accurately represent their actual abilities
Eucharistic	Relating to the act of Holy Communion, where the bread and wine are believed to become Christ's body and blood
eunuch	A castrated male; if the procedure happened before puberty he would remain high-voiced and beardless
gay	Used by Boswell to describe voluntary same-sex relationships, with or without sexual intercourse
hegemonic	Dominant, a leading model

hermaphrodite	A person born with some of the physical attributes of both sexes
heteronormativity	Assumption that male-female sexual activity is the norm
homosexual	A modern and hybrid term applied to same-sex relationships
homosocial	A same-sex relationship that may or may not involve sex
iconography	Pictorial sources
impairment	Physical or mental deficiency
liturgical	Texts relating to the ceremonies of the church or other religions
menarche	Start of menstrual periods
monogamy	Marriage to a single spouse at any one time
monstrosity	Any condition that falls outside boundaries of understanding, or readings of that condition
postpartum	Immediately following the birth of a baby
scholastic	Relating to intellectual exchange, often contrasted with practice on the ground
secular	Relating to the laity rather than the clergy
sodomy	Anal sex between men, but could refer to any non-procreative sexual activity in medieval clerical texts
vernacular	Written in the language spoken, rather than Latin

4

Rules: Patriarchy, the Law and Gendered Behaviour

Even if there were 'women at the beginning', medieval society was governed by the rules and customs laid down and enforced by men. 'Patriarchy' is often used as a shorthand term to describe the series of legal and moral codes that combined to subject women – and their property – to the authority of male relatives or, failing these, religious or secular leaders. According to the late feminist pioneer Gerda Lerner, patriarchal structures could be traced back to prehistory, as she outlined in the first of her two key books tracing 'the origins of women's subordination', *The Creation of Patriarchy*, published in 1986. Almost simultaneously (1988), the first part of a two-volume work by Bonnie Anderson and Judith Zinsser, *A History of their Own*, was published and, like Lerner's, started its survey with a discussion of prehistoric and ancient traditions subordinating or empowering women. Since those important milestones were published, the influence of gender history has led to a realization that patriarchal structures also led to the subjection of the young and the very old of both sexes, as well as controlling the lives of those who entered into quasi-familial relationships such as apprentices and servants. That is, class and age also affected patriarchal relations.

Ancient traditions had a persistent afterlife. In the Middle Ages the dominant influences on lawmakers in western and eastern Europe were Biblical (Old and New Testament); and/or derived from ancient Greek and Roman models (which were revived, to some extent, in the renewed interest in political and legal ideals in the twelfth century); and/or a strong thread of 'Germanic' customs that pre-existed Roman rule and were either preserved or modified as different peoples met with and took over parts of the western Roman Empire (Byzantium remained effectively Roman, although successive eastern emperors would issue 'novels' to add to the body of Roman law). A whole series of graduate dissertations on the Germanic law codes emanated in the 1970s and onwards from Rice University in Texas, where Katherine Fischer Drew's influence was and is still felt. Drew's own work on family law in the early medieval codes spanned much of Europe and was published in an arc from the early 1960s to late 1980s, alongside her translations of some of these codes into English. Of course, many parts of medieval Europe long remained untouched by Roman *or* Christian frames of law, particularly in the Celtic world to the West and Scandinavia to the North, and some non-Christian communities, as we shall see, remained virtually **autonomous**.

Laws and customs, no matter what their origin, were far from consistent in their approach to gender relations. The influential Apostle Paul seems to reject hierarchical relations in one of his letters: 'There is neither Jew nor Greek, there is neither slave nor free man, *there is neither male nor female, for you are all one in Christ Jesus*' (Letter to the Galatians, 3.28, my emphasis); yet reinforces them in his first letter to the Corinthians, 14.34 when he states that women should keep silent in the churches. The latter command will be explored in the next chapter on authoritative voices, but the inconsistency between these two statements reflects the dichotomy between encouraging belief (a recruitment drive open to all) and setting down frameworks for the early Church (which mirrored Judaism in its promotion of male leadership). Subsequent commentators on biblical passages (and these came from all three major religions: Christianity, Judaism and Islam) found space to promote their own view of gender relations through selective readings, and as the literate majority in medieval Europe, the clergy/rabbis/imams also had an influential role in helping rulers to draft and redraft laws regulating their people's behaviour. This blurs the line between 'secular' and 'religious' law. It is worth emphasizing the contradictions and inconsistencies visible in surviving legal codes and how they were interpreted, since those contradictions continue to fuel debates about the 'status' or 'position' of women in this period.

Defining Patriarchy and Controlling Women

We need, however, to take a step back and think about what the word 'patriarchy' actually means. In ancient Greek and Roman law, each household, including its slaves and servants as well as family members, was considered to be under the authority of an adult male, in Latin the *paterfamilias*, literally the father of the family. The term 'patriarch' is a combination of Greek terms for father's (patros/πατρος) and rule (archē/αρχή) – and by establishing fathers as leaders in this way, there was no need for the Greek city state, or Roman republic or empire, to concern itself with behaviour or morals within domestic spaces, because these were the responsibility of the male head of the household. Only in exceptional circumstances was a woman able to take and maintain control, usually as a result of the death or incapacity of the patriarch, and only if she herself was of mature age (at least 25).

As the Roman Empire in the West fragmented in the fifth and sixth centuries CE into successor states ruled by non-Roman leaders (the adjective 'Germanic' is often used for these, and even, in earlier scholarship, 'barbarian'), there was a de-centralizing and breakdown of Roman law, and various new codes of laws were issued by the new rulers that both crystallized existing tribal customs and took on a greater or lesser veneer of Roman laws too. Ideas of masculine dominance over women, however, remained tenacious, and the new codes perpetuated the idea of women as intrinsically incapable of ruling over themselves or others (remember the uncontrolled women in Chapter 2?). The most explicit of these was contained in the law code of the Lombard King Rothari, ruling over northern Italy in the mid-seventh century, and made up of nearly 400 clauses. Rothari's clause 204 reads:

> No free woman who lives according to the law of the Lombards … is permitted to live under her own legal control … but she ought always to remain under the control of some man or the king.

That is, women of all ages were permanently subject to the protection of a man, and if a woman did not have any adult male relatives who could perform this function, she became a ward of the king instead. From other clauses throughout the Lombard laws, we can see that women were permitted to inherit and own property, and were very much protected when it came to their physical well-being, but this control or **mundium** over their freedom of action was pretty much non-negotiable. A woman wanting to sell or give away her property, for example to the Church, had to have the permission of her *mundoald* or guardian written into the transaction, but also had to state that she had suffered no violence from him, i.e. that the transaction was not being made under duress. Medieval documents from Italy that record property transfers – which of course were written with the law in mind – appear to show that the applicability of this law lasted well into the eleventh century, long after the last Lombard kings were ruling in the peninsula, and especially in the south.

The obvious drawback of patriarchal law, as was also apparent in its Roman and Greek precursors, is evident: how to ensure that the guardian, the male head, did not abuse his position. A woman's statement that she had not been coerced into alienating her property could, after all, be subject to duress as well. What happened behind closed doors, however, was not the king's concern unless the person behind that door had no right to be there.

The idea of distinguishing what happened within and outside the household had a long afterlife in legal norms of modern European states. As strong as the push for gender equality before the law may have been in the modern era, there was still a very strong cultural pull in the nineteenth century towards the idea that women should not strive for equality on a male model, but celebrate and cultivate their difference as a positive quality. Many women took this position, in opposition to their campaigning contemporaries. This found its expression in the language of a **public-private** dichotomy, with the male actively pursuing his political life outside the home, whilst the female took care of the domestic environment, maintaining her modesty, having and tending to children and overseeing the day-to-day rhythms of the household (the so-called 'angel of the hearth' model). This was, for all but the most privileged, a complete fiction, but the *idea* of the male economic provider supporting this domestic environment of the family has persisted in the still current pay differentials visible between men and women in the workplace, for all that pay differences according to gender have been made illegal in much of the developed world.

The trope of female modesty also fed into ideas of **separate spheres**. This was a persistent, idealized and ultimately flawed image not only of the lived reality of ancient and medieval life but also of many modern, non-elite households, where the economic imperative for both husband and wife to engage and *collaborate* in paid work broke down the supposed barrier between private and public. Separate spheres, whether enforced by law or a voluntary retreat by women into a space they saw as their own, was an ambivalent analytical category for medievalists. For example, women's retreat into single-sex, monastic spaces could be read either as a convenience for their families (Karl Leyser's classic text on early medieval Germany highlights this use, implying that the women at the centre had little choice in the matter) or as a means to gain the support and companionship of a like-minded group of women (feminist readings of abbesses as role models and mentors for younger women come to mind here, and both shared the language of 'sisterhood'). In a now classic study, archaeologist Roberta Gilchrist was able to demonstrate, using the archaeological technique of access analysis, how the layout of nunneries differed from that of monasteries for men, in particular in the location of their respective dormitories and public spaces, such as the abbot's or abbess's quarters, where they might expect to meet visiting dignitaries. Here, gender's relational quality is paramount: as one moved through the space, the possibilities for different interactions presented and then removed themselves. But this female space was always permeable: male clergy administered the sacraments, the economic status of the house might depend on donors of both sexes, and a novice, however religiously motivated, might well have to leave the convent if it suited her family to marry her off instead. For nuns, queens and chaste wives and daughters, the dormitory or chamber represented the heart of their living space, and was often planned to be the least accessible part of the building or range of buildings in which they lived and worked. By contrast the street, particularly in an urban environment, represented a potentially dangerous space that most women, nevertheless, had to negotiate on a daily basis.

This at least is the standard view, reiterating once more the persistent idea of a distinctly 'feminine' space that corresponds with the private and inaccessible, and feeding into the prevailing ideal of modesty and invisibility. The dense, urban environment in some later medieval cities, however, challenged the possibility of delineating specific zones by their gendered use: men and women lived cheek by jowl, and examining the urban space also highlights that privacy, if it existed at all, was a product of privilege and wealth.

The idea of a 'domestic sphere' was also problematic: when Jo Ann McNamara (see Chapter 2) proposed that the early middle ages had been a time when women could exert power through their familial connections, she certainly did not have in mind a feminine, private space (though the trope of wives influencing their powerful husbands in the chamber has had a life of its own, to the extent that the gender dynamics of interior and exterior spaces are now a subject of study in themselves). Inspired by Gilchrist's work, Felicity Riddy, Leonie Hicks and Amanda Richardson have subjected secular spaces such as urban houses, castles and later medieval palaces to similar types of scrutiny, and have come up with markedly different opinions as to the gendered uses of space. For example, the bed-chamber, seen as a site of privacy and intimacy, has been recast as a place where the most privileged were able to meet with their lord or lady, the access granted to them a special sign of favour. Jinty Nelson, whose own work explored the powerful women in Frankish courts (including those whose power derived from their birth, rather than any specific office or function), highlights the hazards of trying to write any history of 'private life' shaped by modern assumptions of separateness, and is roundly critical of the assumption that 'a universal, commonsensical category of the "private" [can] be equated with the "inside", domestic sphere'. Yet it is instructive to note that even as recently as 2013, Isabel de Val Valdivieso (see *Ser mujer*, in the Appendix), reflecting on trends in Spanish medieval historiography, pointed out that the idea of separate spheres was still a very strong theme running through studies of medieval women in Spain.

Using Medieval Laws in Modern Struggles

Despite the fact that law codes are, by definition, statements of what *should* happen rather than what actually *did* happen, the picture of gender relations that they conveyed convinced many early scholars and campaigners to focus on historical legal frames as they explored women's rights and the origins of later oppression. At the same time, early studies of medieval law codes might touch on issues of family law without being explicitly interested in the rights of women. Legal history itself was a backbone of modern state formation, and so we find scholars exploring the status of women not (or not only) to promote women's rights, but perhaps more accurately as a measure of how 'enlightened' a particular period was in its treatment of the legally disabled sex. Pioneering Byzantine historian Georgina Buckler, for example, published a study of women in Byzantine law in 1936, just as modern Greece was developing its Civil Code (issued in 1940). Wardship, the right of the ruler to control of a woman's future in the absence of close family (and thus a version of the *mundium*), would have a long history in different parts of Europe. The English *Magna Carta* in 1215, for instance, includes a concession that widows would not be forced to remarry, a clause seeking to end the practice of kings marrying off wealthy heiresses whose wardship had fallen to them. In his classic study of *Magna Carta*, first published in 1961, English historian J. C. Holt proudly declared that this was 'one of the first great stages in the emancipation of women'.

The legal disablement of women also attracted the attention of campaigners for female emancipation from the eighteenth century onwards. In France, Olympe de Gouges responded in 1791 to the rhetoric of 'liberté, egalité, fraternité (liberty, equality, *brotherhood*, my emphasis)' in the French constitution with her *Déclaration des droits de la femme et de la citoyenne*, in which she called for laws to be made *by* and *for* men and women equally. She did not cite historical examples, but later writers such as Florence Buckstaff in the United States realized the potential of appealing to historical precedents, and this led to studies asking how historical laws had treated women. The German legal historian Gotthold Bohne, for example, published a short essay, 'The position of women in civil and criminal law in the Italian statutes', in 1926. (Germany's own path to female emancipation was somewhat chequered, and complicated by both Nazi-era retrenchment and the post-war division of Germany into East and West.) The Italian civil code, published in 1865, granted unmarried Italian women their legal majority, but the continued subjection of married women to their husbands perhaps prompted Italian historian Diego Bellacosa to publish a study of the *mundium* in medieval southern

Italy in 1906. Only in 1919 were married women in Italy granted a separate legal, and thus economic, identity. In France they had to wait until 1936.

Buckstaff herself published a pioneering article in 1893 on the situation of married women under Anglo-Saxon law, and many later works on medieval women, too, have taken legal frameworks as their starting point in illustrating the subjection of women to patriarchal structures. Pauline Stafford revisited Buckstaff's work when assessing whether and how the legal status of women changed in England between the Anglo-Saxon and Norman periods, focusing particularly on the perception, which she critiques, that prior to 1066 a 'golden age' had existed. Suzanne Fonay Wemple's study of medieval Francia, on the other hand, highlighted the stark fact that the penalties for injuring or killing women in Frankish law codes (there were several) were dependent on whether that woman was of childbearing age.

This highlights a key point about gender and medieval laws: as Lisi Oliver has highlighted, substantive portions of the early medieval law codes were concerned with bodies and sexuality – a father's concern to hand on property depended on knowing that he was the father of his wife's offspring; owners of an estate needed to ensure their workers, free or not, were not injured or encouraged to run away; interpersonal violence could escalate if not regulated with compensation tariffs. Returning then to the Frankish example, a woman's fertility, rather than her own personhood, was the thing of high value here, and several law codes shared the central concern over the reproductive capacity of women's bodies. Penalties were levied for killing a foetus, and regulated not only injuries to women (including shaming them by touch or verbal abuse, or even by stealing their clothes whilst bathing) but also the rights of men over their wives' bodies.

Adultery looms large in the laws, defined not by infidelity (men could have any number of 'natural' offspring by other women, including slaves), but by sleeping with another man's wife. The husband in some codes had the right to kill both partners without any penalty for the killing being levied – rape, too, was governed by a similar principle. Eventually the Church would step in to regulate such matters, but these early laws give a strong sense that women were viewed almost as a commodity. Indeed, an early essay by Diane Owen Hughes traces the evolution in the ancient and medieval Mediterranean world from 'bride price', a payment made to the wife's family on her betrothal and marriage, to dowry, a transfer of property with the bride to her new husband (and, by extension, to his family). Did this signify a rise in the status of the woman at the centre of the transaction? Hardly – it simply shifted the emphasis to how costly it might be to have daughters instead of sons, and left many daughters without dowries in a vulnerable position if they wanted to marry. This is a good example of the 'patriarchal continuum', defined by Judith Bennett as the continued oppression of women (and other subordinate groups) even as legal, economic and social conditions appear to change over time (discussed further below in Chapter 6).

The law maintained its fascination for later feminist historians of the central and later middle ages. In a first foray into feminist scholarship, the French journal *Cahiers de Civilisation Médiévale* featured a special issue on women and law, published in 1977, and included French-language studies on Byzantium and (still a rarity) eastern Europe. The Christian 'reconquest' of Spain from Muslim rule in the eleventh and twelfth centuries generated local law codes in cities and regions that set out beneficial terms for Christian settlers willing to come and populate newly conquered areas, and Heath Dillard explored the gendered implications of some of these Christian texts in her *Daughters of the Reconquest*, finding that women were able to benefit from the vital need for their reproductive capacities. More recently, Miriam Shadis has highlighted that the end of Visigothic rule did not signal the disappearance of Visigothic influence over legal status, for all that most of Iberia came under Muslim domination, and so when Christian rule reasserted itself in the twelfth century, we see female rulers benefiting from vestiges of Visigothic law that (like Lombard law in Italy) had permitted women to inherit alongside their brothers. Law codes from individual city states in Italy from the thirteenth century onwards, heavily influenced by the study of Roman law at the newly emerging universities of Bologna and Naples, have been studied mainly in Italian language publications thus far, particularly by Maria Teresa Guerra Medici. Guerra Medici herself summarized some of her arguments in English in a collection of essays published in Italy in 2004. The key thing to note about both the Spanish and Italian cases is

the fragmented nature of legal frameworks – each city territory in northern Italy had its own set of statutes, most cities in Spain had their sets
of *fueros* or customary laws, which might or might not become rolled
into the laws of the various kingdoms of the Iberian peninsula. Southern
Italy, by contrast, was politically united under successive waves of rulers,
and Emperor Frederick II's laws of 1231 incorporated earlier statutes on
women's legal status. The influence of Italy on the Adriatic region is well
known, and Susan Mosher Stuard has explored legal rights in medieval
Dubrovnik.

There is no doubt that in terms of quantity, the 1980s and 1990s
represent a high point in studies of particular legal frameworks across
Europe. To the studies noted above we could add the work of Judith
Herrin and Averil Cameron on Byzantium, Gavin Hambly and the late
Fatima Mernissi on Islamic women, and that of Fiona Harris-Stoertz on
legal frameworks for pregnancy and childbirth. Although such studies
continue to be published, scholars have increasingly recognized that law-
based studies could only reflect the ideals of the lawmakers, rather than
the realities of their subjects' lives. Work has therefore increasingly turned
to how such laws played out in the settlement of disputes in and outside
court rooms.

Religious Laws

So far we have discussed the use of laws issued by secular rulers, but
women's and men's lives were also conditioned and controlled by religious laws deriving their authority from the Old and New Testaments
of the Bible for Christians (which evolved into **canon** law), the Torah
and its commentaries (Mishna and Talmud) for Jews, and the Koran
for Muslims. The competing claims of secular and religious law often
led to confusion, particularly around rules for marriages: Niki Megalommati has recently highlighted how this played out in Byzantium,
for instance. Indeed, many secular rulers were advised by clerics on how
to frame their law codes according to Christian principles. A common
thread running through all three major religions, however, was the secondary (but nonetheless complementary) role of women within their

communities' religious lives. This drew upon the biblical depiction of the creation of man and woman: man is created first, from the dust in the ground (Genesis 2:7), but then we wait several verses before it occurs to God that 'It is not good for the man to be alone' (2:18), and further delay before woman is created from man's rib (2.22). By this time, Adam has named all the animals and birds, i.e. by naming things in the world he already has a head start when it comes to claiming power and knowledge.

The inherently patriarchal structures of Judaism, Christianity and Islam, all sharing a version of this creation story, adapted it in different ways, thus providing fertile ground for feminist historians to explore how women negotiated spaces for themselves, whether as community leaders or transmitters of the law, particularly to their children. We shall explore how this was expressed in women's own voices in the next chapter, where female writers are considered. Here, though, it is important to highlight that religious laws, like secular ones, were normative frameworks, a starting point for negotiation, certainly, but not inviolable: not for nothing is Avraham Grossman's study of medieval Jewish women titled *Pious and Rebellious*. Furthermore, Simha Goldin has argued that as medieval Europe became ever less tolerant of its Jewish minority in the twelfth and thirteenth centuries, the role of the family in providing social cohesiveness increased in importance, with a concomitant (and not entirely welcome to all) improvement in Jewish women's status. (This, of course, is a somewhat modified form of 'separate spheres' in emphasizing women as the core of the family and home.) Yossef Rapoport has focused on late medieval Muslim society in the Middle East to demonstrate that the patriarchal ideals of marriage within Islam, and in particular the uneven balance between the right of husbands and wives to initiate divorce, were regularly challenged in cases he has found from the cities of Jerusalem, Cairo and Damascus. In particular, by focusing on economic status, he has been able to find a stratum of women who were able to support themselves through work, undermining the patriarchal idea of dependence that underpinned marital relations.

Turning to the Christian community, there were multiple attempts from the eleventh century onwards to codify the confusion of rules that had emerged from numerous Councils of bishops from the early church onwards into a **canon** that could be agreed to by all. That religious laws were regularly broken (or at least, expected to be) is evidenced by another set of texts, the penitentials, which instructed Christian priests how to respond to sinful behaviour with a series of ever more serious penances and punishments. James Brundage has explored both the canon law and penitential material in a huge work, still not eclipsed, that emphasized the difficulty of maintaining a uniform approach to such matters. In the process of rationalizing the canon law, and increasing the authority of the Pope as the head of the Christian community (in the West, at least), different practices and norms emerged that were increasingly labelled as **heresy**. Whilst earlier scholarship saw heretical groups such as the Cathars in southern France and Italy as providing a less oppressive space for women, it is now recognized that writing about the participation of women was a stock way of *attacking* such groups.

Regulating Men

Whilst many medieval texts, religious and secular, discussed women's behaviour explicitly, enabling historians to trace the boundaries that they were not expected to transgress, they did so because women were quite clearly Not-Men, not part of the group that established the rules, that is they were defined by what they *were* but also by what they were *not*. As we have seen, religious and medical discourse understood women to be Not-Quite-Men, a flawed or incomplete version of Man, created second, destined to be subjected simply because of what they represented: sex and sexuality. From this we say that men were not **sexed** – in the texts at least – in quite the same way as women. Yet to accept this and move on reinforces the idea that gender analysis is basically a 'women's issue' and one that need not concern men. It enables senior, mostly male opponents of feminist history, such as Allen Frantzen, to attack, or duck out of critically engaging with, gender work that exposes and challenges the idea of incontestable male privilege as the normal state of affairs. Returning to medieval normative sources, a closer look at how they present male authority can reveal some of the assumptions and the ways in which boys were trained into their appropriate positions.

What is striking about turning a gendered lens onto boyhood and manhood was its effect of pointing up how oppressive social expectations could be: several of the chapters in a collection on medieval masculinity, published in 1999, examined how some well-known elite medieval males such as Alfred the Great of England, and Gerald of Aurillac, struggled to live up to the roles for which they were destined, and had crises of confidence (expressed as bouts of illness, or resistance) centred around making the transition to adult status. That theme was taken up in a sustained manner by Ruth Mazo Karras, whose study examined the early training of boys into acceptable, 'masculine' roles within medieval society, again drawing on approaches used in feminist history that saw socialization as a key source both of gender identity and oppression. Exploring the laws with a fresh eye reveals that men's lives were hedged round with expectations, even if they were not always explicitly set out – to marry, to provide for their heirs, not to succumb to violence (and if they did, facing penalties for inflicting harm on others), not to enter other men's houses uninvited, to ensure their livestock didn't wander, to protect their own wives and not to sleep with those of other men. In addition they were, as we have seen, held responsible for the behaviour of others in their households, and this might include the workers on their estates. And personal injury tariffs also reveal class distinctions alongside gender ones – injuring a semi-free peasant attracted a far lower penalty than injuring a local aristocrat.

Elite men, moreover, were expected not only to obey laws but to enforce them. In some parts of medieval Europe, it is possible to examine records of court cases where, more often than not, the law as written was less in evidence than what was understood to be 'customary' in that particular community. Early examples of such cases, known as *placiti* after the assemblies called to hear them, survive in records from Italy and Iberia from the eighth century onwards; the administrative sophistication of England in the high middle ages (from c.1100) also led to the preservation of numerous cases, in particular from the thirteenth century onwards. Local communities across Europe, whether represented by their **'good men'** (and this *is* usually a gendered distinction, for all that there are isolated cases of women performing a similar function, for example in Spain) or by more formalized juries or councils (made up of the same 'good men', it might be noted), were held accountable to the ruler for offences within their areas, and could be fined collectively if they did not produce a culprit. To be a 'good man' meant upholding one's own reputation, in order to be thought worthy of judging others. And court cases often ended not in a decision either way, but a negotiated settlement that might or might not adhere to the letter of the law. 'Good men' – otherwise known as local officials, concerned neighbours and even wider family members – all had a hand in smoothing over disputes with potential to disrupt the community. This is why, in the massive samples of later medieval court records that survive, for example in England, the extant records of *beginnings* of cases far outnumber those of their *end*.

What is a 'Law'?

If law does not articulate the social reality of men's and women's lives in the Middle Ages, it might be asked what purpose studying medieval law, secular or ecclesiastical, has for the study of medieval gender relations. Primarily, it enables us to see how medieval rulers and bishops, as well as other religious leaders, envisaged the relationships between men and women in their communities, and how these built into a wider social network of relations based on power, property and kin. Laws were, first and foremost, claims to authority and attempts to keep the peace. Does the evidence of medieval law support the idea that medieval society was inherently patriarchal? That is, did the laws converge to produce an oppressive matrix of rules and regulations that contained and controlled women under the 'protection' of men? For early feminists in the modern era, the answer was obvious, which was why they researched the history of the law and challenged the legal landscape of their own day.

For our purposes, however, the normative legal texts are worth mining because they set up frameworks against which we can test how medieval society and culture actually worked, and comparative projects such as *Gender Differences in Legal Cultures*, active since 2000 and hosted by the University of Giessen in Germany, reveal how much there is still to do to bring legal history and gender together in dialogue. Most obviously, many laws articulate male control of most women's lives, but as we have seen, they also implicitly place a burden of expectation on men as well. Adopting and adapting the idea of **hegemonic masculinity**, based on sociologist R. W. Connell's model of how a patriarchal society reproduces and sustains itself, medieval historians are able to reflect on the hierarchical nature of male social relations and how these related to male-female interactions. For all that McNamara posits a shift from class to gender as the organizing principle in medieval society in the central Middle Ages, further work in gendered relations reveals the weakness of assuming all men had the same experiences, and the persistence of class-based norms. There are however some unwritten norms, as we have already touched upon in Chapter 2 – marriage and children are at the centre of many laws; honour has different meanings when applied to men and women; and above all rulers, whether of early kingdoms or later, more sophisticated state structures, claim the right to set standards of life that are often described in moral as well as legal terms. This last point should put us on guard: when we explore laws, they are often contradictory, drawing upon older precedents to gain authority for the ruler and his (or her) legislators. Sometimes a clause is added that seems to be responding to a specific case, and often the mechanisms for enforcement are hinted at – judges, king's representatives, corporal and capital penalties. Provided the idealism of the law is kept in mind – other texts will allow us to see whether it was respected – it is still a useful starting point for examining gender relations in medieval society.

If laws articulate patriarchal norms, how then do acts of transgression disturb the patriarchy of medieval society? The short answer is: 'Hardly at all'. The informal negotiations that surrounded court cases also fuelled the maintenance of norms of power and authority: women's honour was inseparable from that of their male guardians, but also very fragile. One piece of casual but malevolent gossip could ruin a reputation for chastity and modesty, once it achieved credibility through repetition. **Fama**, or common knowledge about one's status or behaviour, occurs sufficiently frequently in accounts of court cases, and chronicles, to suggest that it was a powerful social regulator that spread through word of mouth. Women who chose to remain single, or did not remarry after widowhood, were vulnerable to the assumptions of others regarding their morals, and the recording of such opinions in writing ironically gave authority to such tales. There was a fine line between respectability and being derided as a whore – Beattie's work (see Chapter 3) cites the common idea that whilst men were more likely to be classified in texts by their social status or occupation, women were generally classified by their marital or sexual status: this is why defamation – of men or women – was also treated as an injury.

It is often thought that the rise (or perhaps, recovery) of urbanism throughout medieval Europe in the period c.1050–1250 provided a space for men and women to renegotiate their own social status through migration or economic gains. These shifts were temporary: the legal culture of many later medieval cities became just as oppressive in regulating social behaviour, perhaps even more so, given the more limited geographical sphere that was under surveillance (Jamie Page has explored this issue in some depth for the cities of Germany and Switzerland). In Italy and elsewhere, sumptuary laws sought to control expenditure on the most basic of family events – betrothals, weddings, funerals. Yet this intrusion of the law into the key rituals of family life did not go unchallenged, and the rich whom it targeted were, after all, wealthy enough to pay the fines.

Modelling the Ideals: Late Medieval Conduct Literature

Laws offered an idealized view of male and female behaviour, above all in terms of women's subjection to male control, and supervision of both their property and their modesty. Even if not all girls married, the bulk of written material we have assumed that that was their goal or destination (penitential texts, after all, condemned sex outside of marriage). However, the issue of 'unwritten' assumptions was also raised, and the possibility of informal, and often unwritten norms of behaviour that everyone 'knew' and thus did not need recording, until such norms were transgressed and punishment meted out. This set of unwritten rules has been termed the *habitus* of a given society by philosopher, sociologist and cultural historian Pierre Bourdieu, and has proven a rich idea when examining the social norms of the medieval period. What was and is unwritten governed and continues to govern social relations.

The vast increase in written materials visible from the central and later middle ages, however, led to the writing down of some of these norms, in revival and adaptation of a genre of text that can be termed 'conduct books', although they were not described as such by their authors. There are several surviving conduct books dating to the late fourteenth century, and all assume that the skills a girl would need centred on the care of household and children (see Further Reading for this chapter). Whether they were genuinely intended as usable household manuals or not, they also reveal the tensions for women *and men* in maintaining their appropriate social status, and Glenn Burger suggests that they emerged as a response to the sometimes rabidly misogynist texts that had preceded them (we met one in the *Secrets of Women*, see Chapter 3). A well-run and well-stocked household was, after all, a sign of social status, and women could achieve a positive role in managing their domestic space in this way. Taking a number of forms, and in some cases dealing with issues remarkably similar to late medieval legislation, conduct books sought to assist in the process of socialization of children, by offering handy advice and guidance for women (and, by extension, men) as to correct behaviour, household management, dress and other issues that might cause comment in the wider community. They were written in the vernacular, suggesting they were meant to be used, rather than simply created as literary exercises. It should be emphasized that the *readership* of such texts is very much open to question, but surviving **miscellanies** produced in the vernacular between the thirteenth and fifteenth centuries certainly suggest that household management was not simply a theoretical matter.

Source Hunt: Laws and Gender

Explore the many and varied laws surviving from medieval Europe, including religious laws. What are their primary concerns when dealing explicitly with women, and why do they focus on these aspects?

Early English Laws, online at www.earlyenglishlaws.ac.uk.

English Historical Documents is a series published by Cambridge University Press
and has four volumes covering the period 500–1485, including translated
excerpts of legal texts.

The Burgundian Code, tr. K. F. Drew (Philadelphia, PA: University of Pennsylvania
Press, 1949).

The Laws of the Salian Franks, tr. K. F. Drew (Philadelphia, PA: University of
Pennsylvania Press, 1991).

The Laws of the Salian and Ripuarian Franks, tr. T. J. Rivers (New York: AMS
Press, 1986).

The Lombard Laws, tr. K. F. Drew (Philadelphia, PA: University of Pennsylvania
Press, 1973).

*The Liber Augustalis or Constitutions of Melfi promulgated by the Emperor Frederick II
for the Kingdom of Sicily, 1231*, tr. J. M. Powell (New York: Syracuse University
Press, 1971).

Later laws were issued by individual city states in the north of Italy, and a limited
sample is published in *Medieval Italy: Texts in Translation*, ed. Katherine L.
Jansen, Joanna Drell and Frances Andrews (Philadelphia, PA: University of
Pennsylvania Press, 2009).

The Visigothic Law Code (Forum Iudicum), tr. S. P. Scott at Library of Iberian
Resources Online (LIBRO): http://libro.uca.edu/vcode/visigoths.htm.

R. Thurneysen et al, *Studies in Early Irish Law* (Edinburgh: H. Figgis, 1936).

Canon law: the Medieval Canon Law Virtual Library, online at http://web.
colby.edu/canonlaw/ (but most linked texts are in their original Latin).

The Internet Medieval Sourcebook has a whole page of links to translated law
excerpts: http://legacy.fordham.edu/Halsall/sbook-law.asp.

Jewish laws on family life summarized by Avraham Grossman at the Jewish
Women's Archive: http://jwa.org/encyclopedia/article/halakhic-decisions-
on-family-matters-in-medieval-jewish-society.

Key Reading

J. A. Brundage, *Law, Sex and Christian Society in Medieval Europe* (Chicago, IL:
Chicago University Press, 1987).

G. Lerner, *The Creation of Patriarchy: The Origins of Women's Subordination*
(Oxford, 1986), esp. Chapter 11.

J. Nelson and A. Del Rio, 'Women and laws in early medieval Europe', in *The
Oxford Handbook of Women and Gender in Medieval Europe*, ed. J. Bennett
and R. Mazo Karras (Oxford: Oxford University Press, 2013), 103–116.

Further Reading

B. Anderson and J. P. Zinsser, *A History of their Own: Women in Europe from Prehistory to the Present*, 2 vols (London: Penguin, 1988).

Book of the Knight of La Tour-Landry, Compiled for the Instruction of His Daughters, ed. T. Wright (London: EETS/Kegan Paul, 1868/1906), digitized at http://name.umdl.umich.edu/KntTour-L.

P. Bourdieu, *Outline of a Theory of Practice* (Cambridge: Cambridge UP, 1977).

G. Buckler, 'Women in Byzantine law about 1100 AD', *Byzantion*, 11 (1936): 391–416.

F. G. Buckstaff, 'Married women's property in Anglo-Saxon and Anglo-Norman law and the origin of common law dower', *Annals of the American Academy of Political and Social Science*, 4 (1893), 233–264.

G. D. Burger, *Conduct Becoming: Good Wives and Husbands in the Later Middle Ages* (Philadelphia, PA: University of Pennsylvania Press, in press 2017).

R. W. Connell, *Masculinities* (Cambridge: Polity Press, 1995).

R. W. Connell and J. W. Messerschmidt, 'Hegemonic masculinity: rethinking the concept', *Gender and Society*, 19 (2005): 829–859.

K. F. Drew, *Law and Society in Early Medieval Europe* (London: Variorum, 1988).

R. Gilchrist, *Gender and Material Culture: The Archaeology of Religious Women* (London: Routledge, 1997).

S. Goldin, *Jewish Women in Europe in the Middle Ages: A Quiet Revolution* (Manchester: Manchester University Press, 2011).

The Good Wife's Guide (Le Ménagier de Paris), ed. and tr. G. L. Greco and C. M. Rose (Ithaca, NY and London: Cornell University Press, 2009) supersedes *The Goodman of Paris (Le Ménagier de Paris)*, tr. E. Power (London: Routledge, 1928, repr. Woodbridge: Boydell and Brewer, 2006).

The Good Wife Taught her Daughter, in *The Good Wife Taught Her Daughter, The Good Wyfe Wold a Pilgremage, and The Thewis of Good Women*, ed. T. Mustanoia (Helsinki: Suomalaisen Kirjallisuuden Seuran, 1948). Also online, ed. E. Salisbury, at http://d.lib.rochester.edu/teams/text/salisbury-trials-and-joys-how-the-goode-wife-taught-hyr-doughter.

A. Grossman, *Pious and Rebellious: Jewish Women in Medieval Europe* (Lebanon, NE: Brandeis University Press, 2004).

L. Hicks, *Religious Life in Normandy, 1050–1300: Space, Gender and Social Pressure* (Woodbridge: Boydell, 2007).

D. O. Hughes, 'From brideprice to dowry in Mediterranean Europe', *Journal of Family History*, 3 (1978): 262–296.

C. Kovesi Killerby, *Sumptuary Law in Italy, 1200–1500* (Oxford: Oxford University Press, 2002).

The Laws and Customs of Medieval Croatia and Slavonia: A Guide to the Extant Sources, ed. D. Karbić and M. Karbić and M. Rady (London: UCL, 2013).

R. Mazo Karras, *From Boys to Men: Formations of Masculinity in Late Medieval Europe* (Minneapolis, MN: Minnesota University Press, 2002).

M. T. Guerra Medici, '"City air": women in the medieval city', in *Donne tra medioevo ed età moderna in Italia: ricerche*, ed. G. Casagrande (Perugia: Morlacchi, 2004), 25–51.

Medieval Conduct Literature: An Anthology of Vernacular Guides to Behaviour for Youths, ed. M. D. Johnston (Toronto: University of Toronto Press, 2009).

N. Megalommati, 'Women and family law in Byzantium: some notes', *Historical Reflections/Reflexions Historiques*, 43.1 (2017), 19–32.

Medieval Women and the Law, ed. N. James Menuge (Woodbridge, VA: Boydell, 2000).

J. L. Nelson, 'The problematic in the private', *Social History*, 15.3 (1990), 355–364.

L. Oliver, *The Body Legal in Barbarian Law* (Toronto: University of Toronto Press, 2011).

J. Page, 'Sex and secrecy: a secular prosecution of abortion in fourteenth century Zurich', *The Medieval Journal*, 5 (2015), 81–106.

Y. Rapoport, *Marriage, Money and Divorce in Medieval Islamic Society* (Cambridge: Cambridge University Press, 2005).

A. Richardson, 'Gender and space in English royal palaces, c. 1160-1547', *Medieval Archaeology*, 47 (2003): 131–165.

F. Riddy, 'Looking closely: authority and intimacy in the late medieval urban home', in M. Erler and M. Kowaleski, eds, *Gendering the Master Narrative: Women and Power in the Middle Ages* (Ithaca, NY: Cornell UP, 2003), 212–228.

P. Stafford, 'Women and the Norman conquest', *Transactions of the Royal Historical Society*, 6th series 4 (1994), 221–249.

R. Stone, *Morality and Masculinity in the Carolingian Empire* (Cambridge: Cambridge University Press, 2015).

S. M. Stuard, 'Women in charter and statute law: medieval Ragusa/Dubrovnik', in *Women in Medieval Society*, ed. S. M. Stuard (Philadelphia, PA: University of Pennsylvania Press, 1977), 199–208.

S. F. Wemple, *Women in Frankish Society: Marriage and the Cloister, 500–1000* (Philadelphia, PA: University of Pennsylvania Press, 1985).

Glossary

autonomous	Governed by own community or religious laws
canon	Authoritative, accepted version, often used to describe Church laws as distinct from those of the state
fama	Reputation, 'fame', and the stories and gossip that fuel it
good men	The Latin *boni homines*: men who had a reputation for trustworthiness or other claim to authority within a community, usually but not always belonging to the social elite
habitus	Unconscious norms of behaviour
hegemonic masculinity	See Chapter 3
heresy	Outside the accepted liturgical norms
miscellanies	Collections of different texts in full or extracts
mundium	Control of a male guardian, who might be father, husband, brother, other male relative or, failing these, a representative of the king
public-private	At its most basic form, outside and inside the home
separate spheres	Spaces in theory closed off to the opposite sex (see public-private); in practice the male moves freely between the two
sexed	Defined by biological sex as the primary feature

5

Voices: Authority and Suppression

This chapter confronts one of the major obstacles that faces historians studying gender in medieval culture, the difficulty of finding authentically female voices in the sources. Although we can find women occasionally reflecting on their own lives or the world around them, we largely lack the letters, diaries and creative outputs that historians of later periods can use to access directly the lives of their subjects. After all, the medieval source material, whether from Christian Europe or elsewhere, was almost entirely produced by men, about men and often to be read by other men. Thus our picture of gender relations, particularly before 1200, comes to us from a very narrow group of male and clerical writers, whose act of writing was conditioned by a specific purpose, or to please a specific patron, or intended for a very particular readership who shared the writer's interests and concerns. Chroniclers and historians in the medieval period selected what seemed important to them to set down, not aiming for completeness nor a dispassionate 'truth' – despite often claiming veracity through consulting ancient books or eyewitnesses. Laws expressed both the claim to authority of rulers and religious leaders, and an idealized moral framework for their subjects. Writers of biblical commentaries, or sermons, or saints' lives, wrote as much for their own edification as that of others. Letters, as we shall see, were carefully crafted and designed to show off rhetorical skills. The high culture of Latin (and in Byzantium, Greek) literacy was confined to an educated elite. This might include nuns, whose literacy has formed the subject of recent work, and the occasional laywoman, but for the period up to about 1200, female authors remain a tiny minority in the range of writers that we know about. Of course, it is not only women's voices we are short of – non-elite men, children, peasants, servants and slaves are all under-represented in the European written record, and gender history's search for the disempowered is equally concerned to find these and other groups.

This situation seems to have changed significantly from the thirteenth century onwards, as more literature came to be written in the languages that men and women actually spoke – or at least understood better than Latin. Our sample of medieval women writers increases considerably (as does our record of secular men such as merchants), and some might even be said to give us insights into their lives and how they viewed the world around them. The period from around 1200 to 1500 is seen by some feminist scholars as a golden age of women writing *as* women, that is, not conforming to the male dominated norms of genre and canon, but bringing their own ideas and female perspectives to their writings, the *écriture féminine* described by French philosopher Hélène Cixous and her contemporaries. From this perspective, the later Middle Ages potentially offer a broader, more complete picture of medieval gender relations than the earlier period, but we must not overlook the fact that later medieval writers might still need to find a patron, fulfil a specific purpose, or write their works for an interested readership, and these were issues confronting men as well as women.

In this chapter, however, the focus will be on women, since several processes combined either to silence them, by preventing them from writing in the first place, or to erase them from the historical record, through subsequent treatment of their works as of less 'value' than those of their male counterparts. Gerda Lerner proposed that the education of women was itself an exceptional phenomenon in the premodern era, and that this explains their under-representation in the written sources. The reason for excluding women in this way is often thought to be grounded in the biblical statement by St Paul, that we have already met, in his first letter to the Corinthians, 14:34: 'Let your women keep silence in the churches: for it is not permitted unto them to speak; but *they are commanded* to be under obedience, as also saith the law'. This injunction still underpins the Catholic Church's refusal to admit women to the priesthood, leading feminist scholars such as Karen Jo Torjesen to investigate in detail the evidence for early church structures, and to argue that women were accorded positions of respect and authority from which later, 'reforming' movements gradually excluded them. Thus medieval women wishing to teach or instruct through oral or written means often had to do so in circumscribed ways, and as we shall see, one pathway open to them was to remain anonymous in their writings. Yet even when women were *known* to have written a text, their works might still fade into obscurity through a third process, whereby what they left was deemed by scholars to be less significant or important. This was particularly true of texts that did not seem to have anything to say about the formation of the medieval state and church. We shall explore this process of erasure later in the chapter.

Thus, to follow up on the discussion of patriarchy, medieval women might face significant challenges in being able to leave written accounts of their lives and thoughts, not least a cultural (if not strictly religiously sanctioned) aversion to the idea of a woman instructing others. The women we see transgressing such norms in this chapter did not, ultimately, change the landscape for other women, but may, through their teaching a patronage of other women, have created a space where writing could flourish. One place that much of this activity happened was in female monastic houses, as we shall see presently. We also have to contend with the issue raised in Chapter 2 of the ways in which medieval history as a discipline evolved in the academy: if medieval women's writing engaged with the public, political world, it might attract early and sustained attention that had little to do with the writer's sex. The Byzantine princess and author Anna Komnena is a case in point. Because Anna's work was a biography of her father, the Emperor Alexius I, it has long formed a key source for scholarship on the Byzantine Empire during the eventful eleventh and early twelfth centuries. Georgina Buckler in fact published a biography of Anna in 1929, and this might be said to be the start of Anna's work being read with a gendered lens. There is of course a false distinction here – it is actually quite difficult to find a medieval woman's writing that is *not* in some way politically engaged (here we meet the problematic public-private distinction examined in Chapter 4 in a different form), yet it remains the case that much female authorship went unnoticed and unremarked upon in early histories that focused on the formation of the medieval state.

Access to Education

If patriarchal forces *were* at work to exclude women from writing, how did they operate? I want first of all to explore Gerda Lerner's contention, set out in her 1986 work *The Creation of Feminist Consciousness*, that access to a formal education determined a woman's ability to participate in literate culture. The major problem with this thesis is that it is driven very much by modern preconceptions of literacy as a gateway to knowledge, and an assumption – admittedly driven by the extraordinarily high proportion of surviving medieval Latin texts being written by men – that women were largely excluded from education unless they entered the church as nuns. Indeed, many of our female-authored texts from pre-1200 are by women who embraced this life among other women, and the leadership role *among women* attributed to the Jew Dulcia of Worms (d. 1196) by her husband rabbi Eleazar in his eulogy to her is suggestive of the spaces that might exist within otherwise patriarchal religious structures. Lerner, though, heavily influenced by the ideas of Marx and Engels on the origins of women's oppression, does not have a very high opinion of the religious life, since it does not fit into the model framework of marriage and reproduction that is required to produce a patriarchal society. Like Marx himself, she did not see medieval religion as a positive force, and thus underestimates the positive benefits of a religious life in her work. There are further problems, however, since Lerner's work starts with the definition of a *litteratus* in medieval culture as 'a person with a knowledge of literature (Latin)' that became the mark of a *clericus* or member of the clergy. The opposite, 'illiterate' person, therefore, was a layperson. (The issue of non-Latin literacy, for example within Jewish and Muslim communities in Europe, is not addressed at all.) So the problem here is not access to education in itself, but access to education within lay or secular life. At a sweep, and very early in her book, Lerner therefore closes off discussion of alternative definitions of literacy because they do not fit her overarching thesis of women's exclusion from the literate, educated, clerical world. She does acknowledge the rise of literacy in vernacular languages, associated with mercantile culture from the thirteenth century onwards, but largely dismisses this development as a potential route for female writing. Yet Lerner's work extends from the medieval period to 1870, and one reason she is so pessimistic about the Middle Ages is because she sees the creation of feminist consciousness as a progressive process, intimately linked to access to widening educational opportunities and a growing awareness of the possibilities of effecting social change through networking and sharing texts. Since she wrote, however, there has been a positive explosion of interest in women's writings in medieval Europe (in both Latin and the vernacular languages), and this has enabled a considerable nuancing of her stark viewpoint.

Medieval Literacy

Let's begin with the concept of 'literacy' itself, and in particular Lerner's assertion that it was confined largely to a male, clerical constituency. As scholars such as Brian Stock and (more pertinently) Michael Clanchy have reminded us, literacy skills did not necessarily always encompass both reading and writing. Medieval culture was based far more on **orality** than our own text-based age can begin to understand: memory and custom were sufficient for the transfer of knowledge. Memory, and witnesses to that memory (who often included women), retained an important place in legal proceedings long after it was required by law to commit a transaction, or statement, to writing, and the processes by which medieval memories were transmitted have formed the subject of numerous studies, including Elisabeth van Houts' work on the gender of witnesses, and James Fentress and Chris Wickham's classic book on memory as a social, collective process.

In addition, more people are likely to have acquired a rudimentary ability to read than ever learned to write (Charlemagne (d. 814) is famously depicted struggling to develop his writing skills, since according to his biographer Einhard, he had started too late in life). Writing, in any case, was viewed as a technical skill: we know from thousands of documents, letters and other materials surviving from the medieval period that only a tiny minority of people who composed written texts actually wrote them out as well. This was the job of scribes, who shaped and produced texts that were dictated or drafted by others, and trained others in their profession. We need to keep this immediate filtering process in mind: a 'fair copy' of a particular transaction or conversation would only incorporate the elements that were essential to record. Much of the peripheral discussion, negotiation and intervention by others not directly affected by the transaction would have been left unwritten. But outside the legal sphere, copying texts was something open to men *and* women, and opened the way for both to acquire literacy skills (Michael Riegler and Judith Baskin have highlighted this issue for Hebrew texts, in particular). These issues, as we shall see, all take on a crucial importance when assessing how women came to write.

Whilst access to literacy (defined in medieval Christian Europe, at least, until c.1250 as competence in Latin) was certainly uneven in medieval Europe, it was not primarily divided along lines of sex. In the early Middle Ages, lay literacy may well have been the exception rather than the norm, even among the elite, and the picture is complicated still further by an uneven geographical spread. Where Roman culture remained strongest, e.g. in Italy and Iberia, so too did the practice of committing transactions to writing. Before c.1250, almost all of the written sources from western Europe are in Latin (the exceptions being Anglo-Saxon material from England, and texts emanating from the Jewish and Arabic communities across Europe and Muslim Spain and Sicily). After that date we begin to see more writings in vernacular languages. Lerner rather underplays what was undoubtedly a seismic shift, and states bluntly that 'the majority of women remained illiterate'.

That literacy skills and written, Latin culture may have been over-emphasized as preconditions for women to write is suggested by the fact that there are no major female writers known from medieval Italy – the most literate region in medieval Europe – until the later medieval period. Is it fair, therefore, to read female authors *as women,* thus reinforcing the idea of their exceptionality, or should we instead look at their works as products of their social class, environment and age? Do Katharina Wilson's criteria for literary productivity – education, scholarly idleness, access to materials, some financial independence, patronage and/or religious zeal – apply only to women? Obviously not, yet her final criterion – freedom from repeated pregnancies or childbearing – is, she suggests, a specific requirement. These preconditions lead her to the conclusion, from a different angle to Lerner's, that the most likely place to find a female writer in the Middle Ages would indeed be in a convent. The recent conferences exploring nuns' literacies, along with studies of individual houses, have borne this theory out, and underline the explosion of women's writings in the vernacular even in centres where Latin tuition might still have been available.

What is an Author?

A further complication to be considered is the idea of authorship itself. For if we separate out the physical process of writing, we then have to explore how texts came to be created, and whether they can actually be assigned to one individual. This issue began to be questioned in literary theory in the 1970s and 80s. The French writer Roland Barthes' influential essay on the multiple meanings to be found in every text by each reader, and the absurdity therefore of assigning just one meaning, created and owned by an individual author, had a profound effect on medievalists. After all, Barthes claimed that the sovereignty of the author was a product of modernity, part of the celebration of the individual that the modern era fostered and encouraged. The fact that medieval texts were themselves somewhat generic in nature, drawing upon common themes often from Biblical texts, perhaps dictated by one person and then shaped in the writing up by another, strengthened the argument that such works were also not really attributable to the author whose name they bore. Barthes' assertion, like many we have dealt with so far in this book, was born out of an assumption, which he articulates in another of his works, that medieval writers produced little more than commentaries and expansions of existing texts, what he terms 'the barbarism of the middle ages', rather than anything new or original. To accept his formulation would, at a stroke, eliminate any need to *search* for that original voice. In an age when formulaic norms dominated most medieval writing, with recourses to earlier authorities outweighing the urge to innovate, how useful is it to think of female – or male – writers as 'authors' at all?

Medievalists such as Colin Morris and John Benton early on provided something of a response to Barthes' pessimism, arguing that a sense of self and individuality *was* already present in writings of the twelfth century onwards. Their work has been considerably augmented by the more recent interest in the medieval psyche and emotional life, that again explores self-image and opens the way to considering a particular text as a genuine reflection of the author's intentions. Barbara Newman and John van Engen, in particular, have recently demonstrated that authorial choices and particularism are demonstrable by close reading, and a recognizably feminine and self-confident voice, for example, emerges from such studies. It is probably fair to say that whilst medievalists have acknowledged Barthes' contention, they have not abandoned their interest in individual medieval authors. Rather, the 'literary turn' made historians more aware of the strategies used in the shaping of texts, and led to more attention being paid to anonymous texts that might have been written by women.

It is worth outlining therefore precisely what I mean by the term **author** in this discussion. Here I take it to describe the originator of a work deriving wholly or in part from their own viewpoint or experience. This definition allows for the inclusion of works by named persons, regardless of how original the contents might be (even selecting and excerpting earlier works required a degree of authorial intervention through the choice of works, excerpts and the order they were presented in). Let us pause for a moment to examine some of these individuals and their works.

Finding Female Authors: Dhuoda, Hrotswitha, Anna Komnena

In the work undertaken to recover women authors as part of the broader scheme of restoring women to medieval history, works by (or attributed to) named women were the first to attract early and sustained attention from scholars, keen initially simply to document their existence and make their work accessible. Although the Englishwoman Margery Kempe's *Book*, dictated towards the end of her life in the early fifteenth century and written up by two scribes, was part-published in the sixteenth century, the full manuscript was only rediscovered in 1934, prompting a scholarly edition of 1940 and numerous studies since. We shall return to her, and to another late medieval writer, Christine de Pizan, in the next chapter.

The 1980s and 1990s in particular also saw a plethora of publications that excerpted and anthologized a group of medieval women writers who rapidly became part of a medieval canon (Margery and Christine among them). Some anthologies were however limited by a narrow definition of the term 'writing': Carolyne Larrington in 1995 categorically excluded from her anthology 'documents which are resolutely non-literary or non-narrative'. Viewed charitably, Larrington's choices may have been a response to the fact that some of the early anthologies were concerned with texts *about* as well as *by* women and thus could be viewed as somewhat uncritical in their rush to document women's lives: yet she, too, includes texts by men. More negatively, such definitions set up a false distinction that perpetuated existing frameworks of what was thought 'worthy' of study by literary scholars, and conformed to canons established by a male-dominated academy. Only women who wrote 'literature' made it into this collection. A much more recent volume on British women's writing from 700 to 1500, by contrast, has explored beyond the obvious, named authors, whilst still anthologizing well-known names such as Margery (see McAvoy and Watt in Sources list).

Larrington's stringent rule meant that she excluded the ninth century Latin manual written by the Frankish noblewoman Dhuoda for her son William, which had already appeared in excerpted form elsewhere. This text had already been published in the late seventeenth century, and was re-edited in the nineteenth century within the extensive *Patrologia Latina* collection (see Chapter 1). A French translation by Edouard Bondurand came out in 1887. Whilst there were some subsequent studies on the text, the true significance of Dhuoda's work for feminist scholarship was not realized until a new edition was published in 1975, and attracted the attention of a new generation of scholars. Yet her exceptionality was stressed: Suzanne Wemple in 1981 (see Chapter 4) characterized Dhuoda as an isolated exception to the exclusion of Carolingian women from the intellectual activities of their age, and Katharina Wilson called her an 'enigma'. Indeed, her relative isolation as a woman writer against the background of the renewal of learning that characterized the ninth century Frankish empire might even prompt us to ask 'Did women have a Carolingian Renaissance?' Rather than treat Dhuoda as an exceptional *woman*, therefore, we might want instead to situate her within that period of burgeoning literacy, and see her guidance for William in the broader context of accepted social norms for educating children of the elite. At the same time we must remember that Dhuoda's text was written in exceptional circumstances: she could not impart her advice to William verbally, since for political reasons she was separated from her sons. Subsequent scholarship has sought to mitigate Dhuoda's exceptionality by examining other elements of women's writing in the Carolingian era, and found (perhaps unsurprisingly) a flourishing culture of women's literacy within the religious houses of the Empire.

But mothers also occupied a privileged space among women writers, and exploited this to broaden their sphere of authority. The limitations of focusing on exceptional, named female authors highlighted the fact that those women who left such works came from the elite of medieval society, having access to educational opportunities denied to many within their own class, let alone their own sex. Dhuoda herself, as M. A. Claussen points out, was clearly imbued with knowledge of the Bible and the Rule of St Benedict, both of which she used to structure her work and provide her son with examples of good and bad behaviour.

Gerda Lerner made a further, critical observation in the early 1990s: in order for female writers' works to survive, they had to be known about and read, and in many cases (Dhuoda is a clear example) such writing faded into relative obscurity for many centuries. The nun Hrotswitha of Gandersheim, on the other hand, who was a prolific writer in many **genres**, was known and studied from the fifteenth century onwards, but largely due to being the 'first medieval playwright' (of either sex) and the author of a history of Otto the Great (d. 973) of Germany. In other words, it was her social class – a relative of the Ottonian family – that arguably gave her the authority to write, and it was the content of her texts, not her sex, that was deemed of importance in the early reception and appreciation of her writings. Like Anna Komnena, mentioned earlier, her biography of a 'great man' elevated her importance as a medieval author, regardless of her sex. As she, too, was anthologized in collections of women's writings in the 1980s, her femaleness became the defining factor in her inclusion, and her position of relative *class* privilege faded from view.

Approaches to Authorship

For feminist scholars interested in recapturing and reclaiming women's voices, such concerns led to a re-evaluation of how women and writing intersected in the Middle Ages. The influence of gender studies, with its broader definition of power relations and the intersection of class, age and ethnicity with sex, led to a reconsideration of the importance of education as an entry point to writing medieval texts. It also highlighted the important role of women as patrons and book owners, not just as authors themselves. Gender studies led to a broader understanding of what a female-authored text might look like, and the field widened to include:

- women's voices as transmitted by men (the late medieval *Book* of Margery Kempe, dictated by her to two scribes, is a well-known example);
- women as collaborators and contributors to texts written by men;
- anonymous texts which shared identifiable features with texts by known female writers;
- non-narrative texts, now read in the same way as more 'literary' products: the crafting of letters or witness statements to courts, for instance, could be just as creative as works of fiction and fantasy.

Let us take each of these categories in turn. The first, women's 'writings' transmitted by men, acknowledges that women were not always responsible for writing down the texts that survive. This represents a major departure from the assumption, outlined above, that only educated women with time on their hands (and no children) could leave their thoughts for posterity. What precisely was a female 'writer', then, if her words were recorded by a male scribe? What happened if a text survived only as a copy, not in an **autograph** original? Did this **mediation** in fact create a different authorial voice? One way of dealing with the problem might be to make a distinction between first-person ('I did this') and third-person ('She said this') reports, but the problem with this approach is that medieval authors of both sexes often strove to remove themselves from their texts, or referred to themselves in the third person as a means of displaying modesty and/or a distance from the events they related. The twelfth century abbess, Hildegard of Bingen, is known for a wide variety of writings, including music, medical texts and letters to high-ranking men and women, as well as commentaries on biblical texts which she sets out with a first-person voice, but her religious visions, as even manuscript illustrations make clear, were dictated to a male cleric to be written down. Other spiritual women, too, recounted their experiences to priests and confessors, and again the question has been raised as to the role the latter had in 'shaping' the account. The fourteenth century saint, Catherine of Siena, left numerous prayers, letters and her *Dialogue*, all apparently dictated to a number of scribes. Only their consistent style and conceptual development enables us to be sure that 'the wording is Catherine's own', in the words of Suzanne Noffke. Yet women could also be part of this process of writing down: Alison Beach and Liz Herbert McAvoy have demonstrated the close, female cooperation in the production of texts in the convents of Admont and other houses in Bavaria, and Helfta in northern Germany, in the twelfth and thirteenth centuries respectively, and there is undoubtedly more to be done in terms of linking particular communities in larger, Europe-wide networks.

Almost the reverse of the male **amanuensis** issue, women have been argued to have been prominent and vocal contributors to texts bearing the names of male authors, their contribution only being revealed by close readings. Women as influential collaborators in text production proved a rich seam to mine, in both religious and secular contexts. In an anthology of **hagiographic** texts published in 1992, Jo Ann McNamara and her co-editors commented, 'The deeds and even the voices of women speak to us from the documents ... At least two of the biographies were written by women who knew their subjects. Others reflect the direct testimony of women within the cloister walls.' Frustratingly for us, however, a promised comparison of the male- and female-authored biographies of the Frankish princess St Radegund (d. 587), which might have illuminated how far such texts could be shaped by gender-specific concerns, has never appeared.

But what forms might women's testimony within male-authored texts take? Elisabeth van Houts explored both patronage and memory as ways in which women could shape historical texts. In a ground-breaking study, she took in turn women's contributions as witnesses to chronicles and saints' lives, their crucial role as repositories of memories and family information, and the ways in which material objects, often passed down through female lines, could function as 'pegs for memory'. My own study of a Jewish text written in Italy in the eleventh century drew heavily on her model to explore how objects and places associated with the women of the family functioned as way markers in the (male) author's account. The late Olivia Remie Constable's last major work, *To Live Like a Moor* will surely add to our knowledge of how material, everyday items contributed to both identity (whether of self or others) and remembrance of identity in the fluid religious world of Muslim and Christian Iberia when it is published in early 2018. The material objects that women of all social classes were expected to look after (and particularly the goods they took with them into marriage) might themselves have been passed on down generations (and women's and men's wills show that they were). What items formed 'pegs for memory' and how were they handed down? Surviving wills of men and women list specific, possibly treasured items separately from the bulk of the estate, however modest that might be. In some regions, such as Italy, the will could be followed up with an inventory drawn up when the wishes of the deceased were executed, and a record required of who had got what. How were material items, including books, clothing, jewellery, weapons, pots and pans and household furnishings, distributed in terms of ownership and use? What possibilities for gendered readings does the design and execution of pictures, tools, clothes and household items offer? How might items be re-purposed and reused according to the changing context? Whilst archaeological work on materials deposited in burials has engaged with this question, the potential to incorporate material culture and records of material culture into historical analysis is still somewhat unfulfilled beyond individual case studies, and even in conferences devoted to this theme, the medieval period has only featured sporadically. This is a neglected area of 'text' that would reward further investigation.

This acknowledgement of material culture as a text, and of orality, again reminds us that both men's and women's opportunities to contribute to writing correlate only superficially to the acquisition of literacy skills. Patronage also played an important part: Pauline Stafford was able to demonstrate the interventions of Queens Emma and Edith of England in Latin texts produced at their courts, the one a praise of Emma herself, the other a life of Edith's deceased and saintly husband, Edward. That Emma and her collaborator in the *Encomium Emmae Reginae* chose to produce a Latin text against the background of a multilingual court where English, Danish and Latin were all viable language choices is interpreted by Liz Tyler as a strategic 'lay claim to Latin literary culture' on Emma's part. Of course these were both powerful women, but their power was considerably enhanced by their management of texts.

Thus one obvious element of women's contribution to text, as evidenced by Queen Edith's shaping of Edward's *vita*, might be in their acknowledged role as commemorators of the deceased. Of course, many of these women owed their influence over male writers to their position within the social elite. We might ask again whether class, rather than gender, contributed to their interventions. As custodians of the memory of powerful husbands, however, widows might perpetuate their own importance within the wider family. Their repositories of knowledge might also be based on milestones in their own lives. If mothers, the births (and deaths) of their own children might have functioned as way markers in their memories of other events. If we look at a document such as the diary of the Florentine merchant Gregorio Dati (d. 1435), it is impossible to imagine that he could have kept up with the frequent births and deaths of his children without input from his four known wives (he was a serial monogamist, as well as having casual sexual relations outside of his home).

But the possibilities of extending the definition of women's writing do not stop there. Starting from examples of female authors (Anna and Hrotswitha again) and female collaborators and patrons, Jinty Nelson asked in 1991 whether in fact there is an identifiably female perspective in the ways in which their texts were composed, and whether this might enable a fresh appraisal of anonymous texts or those generally attributed to male authorship. Wilson had already suggested that female authors often depicted female characters in their texts more frequently, more sympathetically and more convincingly than male authors. Her conclusions, however, were based on texts known to be written by women, and

Nelson identified three features that might point towards female control and authorship of the text:

* an experimental or mixed form that might include oral alongside written source material (reminiscent of Cixous' *écriture féminine* that rejected linear, narrative forms);
* a heightened sensitivity and attention to family politics of the elite;
* more extensive attention on the role of women in those politics.

Crucially, Nelson stressed that *all three* features needed to be present, and more texts explored, before a cast-iron case could be made for gender-specific authorial strategies, a warning that subsequent readers of her influential article have often ignored. Claussen, for example, asked whether Dhuoda's 'immediacy and emotion' have anything to tell us about how women read and write, succumbing to a gendered stereotype that codes emotional language as female. And an interest in 'family stories' alone was not sufficient to justify claiming female authorship, for male authors were just as interested in dynastic histories. Rather more carefully, Rosamond McKitterick took on the question of anonymity in her study of women's literacy in early medieval Francia.

Anonymity in a medieval text might speak of the author's own desire that the words speak for themselves, or might even bolster the idea that the 'author' did not exist in the medieval period. Humility was, after all, a desirable trait in male clerical writers, and appears in numerous prologues and prefaces as a claim not to be up to taking on a writing task demanded by a patron or religious house (the so-called 'humility *topos*'). Yet they still wrote. How then did women, enjoined to 'keep silence' in the Bible, participate in writing against a background of patriarchy? Again: they still wrote, sometimes employing exactly the same stance of humility or, in the case of the eighth century nun Huneberc/Hugeberc, disguising their authorship (of two male saints' lives) in an elaborate cryptogram only deciphered in 1931. Dhuoda repeatedly belittles herself even as she claims William's attention.

We have come a very long way, therefore, from a narrow sample of named, female writers, and instead explored how medieval texts reward a gendered approach that does not start with hard and fast categories of inclusion and exclusion. This has much wider application: Tova Rosen, for instance, explores the 'silencing' of women in medieval Hebrew literature, but through her feminist readings reveals gendered assumptions that still hold true today, and through highlighting women's voices, however muffled, she seeks to show how such '"illegitimate" utterances of the "other" threaten to undermine the dominant discourse' of men. Her work brings us to a final theme in this chapter on writing and authority, the ways in which medieval women's voices, even when captured in texts, have still been elided and omitted by the scholarly practices of the modern age.

Processes of Exclusion and Excision: Women's Letters

In the introduction to this book, I highlighted Kathryn Maude's important essay on the obscuring of important work by female scholars in the nineteenth and early twentieth centuries on editions of medieval texts. Her essay builds on Gerda Lerner's contention that women's intellectual labours are obscured and forgotten from one generation to the next, so that scholars such as Anglo-Saxonist Elizabeth Elstob, active in the eighteenth century, need to be 'rediscovered'. But it also points up the problems of how work within and outside the academy is validated by a narrow canon of what is considered 'important', which numerous scholars, male and female, have consciously or subconsciously perpetuated across generations of teaching. Here, I want to take as an example a genre of texts in which women's voices occur without apology, letter-writing, and use it to expose the ways in which editing practices and subsequent historiography have contributed to a mythology that gender history in its narrowest sense of male-female relations is unviable because women are 'invisible' in the sources.

I suggested earlier that maintaining a category such as 'literary texts' is an exclusionary practice, ignoring texts that are crafted and can be narrative even if they survive in a form, such as a charter or letter, that is not immediately thought of as such. Here I address another category, 'historical texts', and suggest that the masculinist agenda of tracing early state formation and politico-legal structures that drove the editing of texts was similarly exclusionary, and even where women's voices are apparent they are not discussed or signalled in the scholarly apparatus such as indices and **rubrics**.

How does this play out in the case of letters? Introducing their collection of medieval women's letters in translation, Karen Cherewatuk and Ulrike Wiethaus suggest that women had to 'write at the margins of a realm staked out by male authors'. Letters are also not unproblematic sources. Indeed, they share many of the issues we have just rehearsed for longer texts – is a woman's letter redacted by a scribe really 'hers'? What about one reported in a separate text? Marcelle Thiébaux stresses that letter-writing was a 'normal' form of female authorship: it required no apology, even if it might be similarly circumscribed by considerations of class, access to literacy or the resources to dictate it to a scribe (raising the issue of mediation again). For all that there is now a huge repository of items at the online *Epistolae* resource, medieval letters are a still underexploited form of women's writing.

One reason for this under-exploitation, I suggest, relates straight back to Gerda Lerner's point about access to education and the privileging of certain forms of knowledge. The interests of historians in the latter half of the nineteenth century were focused on rather different issues than those of a century later, and this manifests itself in a failure to pay attention to certain types of evidence for women's agency. I take as an example the editorial strategies of collections such as the *Monumenta Historicae Germanica* (*MGH*, See Chapter 1) (and the volumes cited here were all initially produced in the nineteenth or early twentieth centuries). These have in fact disguised the extent of female letter-writing, at least for the early Middle Ages (and probably for the later period too): in letter collections associated with men, such as Charlemagne's biographer, Einhard, or Alcuin, or St Boniface, or Abbot Lupus of Ferrières, the contents pages totally ignore the presence in such collections of their *female* correspondents.

Similarly, the life of the Frankish bishop, St Desiderius of Cahors (d. 655), embeds within its pages three letters stated to be from his mother, Herchenfreda, the first an exhortation to live a God-fearing life, the second dealing with news and practical matters such as what Desiderius wants sent

to him (and this explicitly reveals the ways in which female correspondents provided help and support for male writers), and the third, a heartfelt
plea from a 'distressed mother' to Desiderius to keep himself safe after the
murder of his brother, Rusticus, and death of his other brother, Siagrius.
These three letters are not only buried in this text, but are also completely
overlooked in the separate *MGH* volume (1892) that collects and publishes Desiderius's correspondence, for all that the collection there features
letters *to* him as well as *by* him. Does his mother not count as an important correspondent? Did the editors omit the letters because they were only
reported – albeit transmitted there in apparent entirety – in the *vita*? We
are not told, but we might surmise that letters from an anxious mother,
whose authority over her son is evident from her language, did not 'fit' the
image of the bishop himself as a figure of authority. The *vita* itself could
not be redacted to remove Herchenfreda – this would have breached editorial standards – but it is quite clear that a deliberate choice was made not
to include her voice in the letters volume. (She does not currently appear in
Epistolae either, though that site does state that only 800 or so of the 2000
letters being translated are currently online.) It is possible that this is simply
an accident of the editorial process – the *MGH* edition of the *vita* came out
a decade after the letter collection. Before we assume that the editor of the
letters may not have *known* the life, however, we should note that it had
already appeared in volume 87 of the *Patrologia Latina* (*PL*, see Chapter 1)
series (published in 1851). Such suppressions have had a knock-on effect
in modern scholarship: the *authority* of such collections as the *Monumenta*
means that there has been little questioning, up to now, of the editorial
policies that lay behind them. Yet these editions also drive the selection of
texts for translation, and their presentation in student textbooks, perpetuating ideas of what survives and what is important. Completing Herchenefreda's story, it should be noted that the *PL*, in both its 19th-century print
edition and 1990s online version, heads this life up as 'Desiderius, bishop
of Cahors, and Herchenefreda his mother'. The *MGH*, therefore, seems
to have deliberately omitted any attention to gendered relations as a key
element in the lives of these 'great men'. The importance of maternal piety
in male saints' lives, after all, had a long history stretching back through St
Augustine's mother Monica, the Emperor Constantine's mother Helena
and ultimately to the Virgin Mary herself.

There is an intriguing paradox at the heart of considering medieval women as writers: although their role as repositories of knowledge of family connections gave women a voice in other texts, very few of the women known to have left us writings of their own were doing so within the heart of family life. Contrary to the idea of the mother as an educator, which did offer authority, most female authors whose works survive are not known to have been mothers, and many had removed themselves from the secular concerns of family altogether, or wrote only when their involvement became less intense, or their childbearing years were well and truly over. Even Dhuoda herself was writing in the absence of her husband and sons. Anneke Mulder-Bakke has explored this intersection of age and life cycle: strikingly, many female writers were older women, and age was also an asset when drawing upon memories of generations to enrich the historical narrative.

Growing 'old' was again a relative phenomenon: archaeological evidence reveals that by their forties, men and women might show distinct signs on their bones of a life of hard labour, or malnutrition, or injuries that had healed only partly. Deborah Youngs explored gender and the life cycle in a ground-breaking book that has since inspired further reflections on how men and women experienced growing up and growing old in quite markedly different ways, and Shulamith Shahar has explored both ends of the age spectrum with books on childhood and old age. In between, it is clear, was the prime of life: we have already met the valorization of women of childbearing age in nakedly fiscal terms in early medieval Frankish laws. For both men and women, the 'prime of life', theorized by numerous medieval texts, has yet to be fully explored as it played out in practice. Part of the problem here lies in the fact that this particular life stage represented the invisible norm, less worthy of comment than whitened hair and beards, bent backs, failing eyes or missing teeth. Although we have plenty of descriptions of medieval men and women outlining their beauty, physicality and markers such as height, colouring and other physical features worthy of note, the origins and generic quality of some of these would bear further investigation. But this discussion of women writers leads us into the subject of identity – did they write *as women*, as French theorists Hélène Cixous, Julia Kristeva and Luce Irigaray believed (see Cavallaro) – or are we as scholars assuming that this is how they would have identified themselves? The question of identity lies at the heart of gender history, and it is to this we now turn.

Source Hunt: Women's Voices in the Text

Starting with writings attributed to named, medieval women, how wide a range of materials have some element of female authorship (patronage, collaboration) or convey women's voices (letters are a good place to look)? Compare texts *by* women with texts *about* them. Are there differences in style or emphasis?

Sources

E. Amt, ed., *Women's Lives in Medieval Europe: A Sourcebook* (London: Routledge, 1993, 2nd edition 2010).

Anna Komnena, *Alexiad*, tr. E. R. A. Sewter (Harmondsworth: Penguin Classics, 1969).

Encomium Emmae Reginae [Praise of Queen Emma], ed. and tr. A. Campbell and S. Keynes (Cambridge: Cambridge University Press, 1998 [1949]).

K. Cherewatuk and U. Wiethaus, eds, *Dear Sister: Medieval Women and the Epistolary Genre* (Philadelphia, PA: University of Pennsylvania Press, 1993).

Dhuoda, *Handbook for William: A Carolingian Woman's Counsel for her Son*, tr. C. Neel (Washington, DC: CUA Press, 1991).

P. Dronke, ed., *Women Writers of the Middle Ages* (Cambridge: Cambridge University Press, 1984).

Epistolae: Medieval Women's Letters, at https://epistolae.ccnmtl.columbia.edu.

L. Herbert McAvoy and D. Watt, eds, *The History of British Women's Writing I: 700–1500* (London: Palgrave, 2012).

C. Larrington, ed., *Women and Writing in Medieval Europe* (London: Routledge, 1995).

J. A. McNamara, J. E. Halborg and E. G. Whatley, eds, *Sainted Women of the Dark Ages* (Durham, NC: Duke University Press, 1992).

M. Thièbaux, ed., *The Writings of Medieval Women* (New York: Garland, 1987; revised and expanded edition 1994).

Two Lives of Charlemagne, tr. David Ganz (London: Penguin, 2008).

K. M. Wilson, ed., *Medieval Women Writers* (Athens, GA: University of Georgia Press, 1984).

Women Writing Latin from Roman Antiquity to Early Modern Europe, II: Medieval Women Writing Latin, ed. L. Churchill, P. Brown and J. E. Jeffrey (New York: Routledge, 2012).

Key Reading

R. Barthes, 'The death of the author' [1967], reprinted in *Image, Music, Text* (New York and London: Wang/Fontana, 1977).

B. Holsinger, 'The four senses of Roland Barthes', in his *The Premodern Condition: Medievalism and the Making of Theory* (Chicago, IL: Chicago University Press, 2005).

N. Clarke, 'Elizabeth Elstob (1674–1752): England's first professional woman historian?', *Gender and History*, 17 (2005), 210–220.

G. Lerner, *The Creation of Feminist Consciousness from the Middle Ages to 1870* (Oxford and New York: Oxford University Press, 1986).

J. L. Nelson, 'Gender and genre in women historians of the early middle ages', in *L'historiographie médiévale en Europe*, ed. J.-P. Genet (Paris: CNRS, 1991), 149–163; reprinted in J. L. Nelson, *The Frankish World, 750–900* (London: Hambledon, 1996).

Further Reading

A. I. Beach, *Women as Scribes: Book Production and Monastic Reform in Twelfth-Century Bavaria* (Cambridge: Cambridge University Press, 2004).

P. R. Brown, L. A. McMillin and K. M. Wilson, eds, *Hrotsvitha of Gandersheim: Contexts, Identities, Affinities and Performances* (Toronto: University of Toronto Press, 2004).

G. Buckler, *Anna Comnena: A Study* (Oxford: Oxford University Press, 1929, repr. 2000).

The Cambridge Companion to Medieval Women's Writing, ed. C. Dinshaw and D. Wallace (Cambridge: Cambridge University Press, 2003).

Dani Cavallaro, *French Feminist Theory: An Introduction* (London and New York: Continuum, 2003.

M. T. Clanchy, *From Memory to Written Record: England 1066–1307* (3rd ed., Chichester: Wiley, 2013).

M. A. Claussen, 'Fathers of power and mothers of authority: Dhuoda and the *Liber Manualis*', *French Historical Studies*, 19.3 (1996), 785–810.

J. Fentress and C. J. Wickham, *Social Memory* (Oxford: Basil Blackwell, 1992).

Gender and Material Culture in Historical Perspective, ed. M. Donald and L. Hurcombe (Basingstoke: Palgrave Macmillan, 2000).

Gendered Voices: Medieval Saints and their Interpreters, ed. C. M. Mooney (Philadelphia, PA: University of Pennsylvania Press, 1999).

V. Greene, 'What happened to medievalists after the death of the author?' in *The Medieval Author in Medieval French Literature*, ed. V. Greene (New York: Palgrave Macmillan, 2006), pp. 205–227.

L. Herbert McAvoy, 'Anonymous texts', in *The History of British Women's Writing, 700–1500*, ed. L. Herbert McAvoy and D. Watt (Basingstoke/New York: Palgrave Macmillan, 2012), 160–168.

L. Herbert McAvoy, '"O der lady, be my help": women's visionary writing and the devotional literary canon', *Chaucer Review*, 51 (2016), 68–87.

R. McKitterick, 'Women and literacy in the early middle ages', in her *Books, Scribes and Learning in the Frankish Kingdoms, 6th to 9th Centuries* (Aldershot: Variorum, 1994).

G. K. McLeod, 'Humility topos', in *Women in the Middle Ages: An Encyclopaedia*, ed. K. M. Wilson and N. Margolis (Westport, CN: Greenwood Press, 2004), 448–452.

A. Mulder-Bakke, 'The metamorphosis of woman: transmission of knowledge and the problems of gender', in *Gendering the Middle Ages*, ed. P. Stafford and A. Mulder-Bakke (Special issue of *Gender and History*, 12.3 (2000), reissued as a book, Oxford: Blackwell, 2001), 642–664.

J. L. Nelson, 'Dhuoda', in *Lay Intellectuals in the Carolingian World*, ed. J. L. Nelson and P. Wormald (Cambridge: Cambridge University Press, 2007), 106–120.

B. Newman, 'Annihilation and authorship: three women mystics of the 1290s', *Speculum*, 91 (2016), 591–630.

S. Noffke, 'The writings of Catherine of Siena: the manuscript tradition', in *A Companion to Catherine of Siena*, ed. C. Muessig, G. Ferzoco and B. Mayne Kienzle (Leiden: Brill, 2012), 295–338.

Nuns' Literacies in Medieval Europe: The Hull Dialogue, ed. V. Blanton, V. O'Mara and P. Stoop (Turnhout: Brepols, 2013).

E. H. Pagel, 'What became of God the mother? Conflicting images of God in early Christianity', *Signs*, 2 (1976), 293–303.

M. Riegler and J. Baskin, '"May the writer be strong": medieval Hebrew manuscripts copied by and for women', *Nashim: A Journal of Jewish Women's Studies and Gender Issues*, 16 (2008), 9–28.

T. Rosen, *Unveiling Eve: Reading Gender in Medieval Hebrew Literature* (Philadelphia, PA: University of Pennsylvania Press, 2003).

S. Shahar, *Childhood in the Middle Ages* (London and New York: Routledge, 1992).

S. Shahar, *Growing Old in the Middle Ages: Winter Clothes us in Shadow and Pain* (New York: Psychology Press, 2004).

P. Stafford, *Queen Emma and Queen Edith* (Oxford: Blackwell, 1997).

B. Stock, *The Implications of Literacy* (Princeton: Princeton UP, 1983).

S. A. Stofferahn, 'Changing views of Carolingian women's literary culture: the evidence from Essen', *Early Medieval Europe*, 8 (1999), 69–97.

K. J. Torjesen, *When Women were Priests: Women's Leadership in the Early Church and the Scandal of their Subordination in the Rise of Christianity* (San Francisco, CA: Harper, 1993).

E. M. Tyler, 'Talking about history in eleventh-century England: the *Encomium Emmae Reginae* and the court of Harthacnut', *Early Medieval Europe*, 13 (2005), 359–383.

J. van Engen, 'Authorship, authority and authorization: the cases of Abbot Bernard of Clairvaux and Abbess Hildegard of Bingen', in *Shaping Authority*, ed. S. Boodts, J. Leemans and B. Meijns (Turnhout: Brepols, 2016), 325–362.

E. van Houts, *Memory and Gender in Medieval Europe, 950–1200* (Basingstoke: Palgrave, 1999).

E. van Houts, 'Women and the writing of history in the early Middle Ages: the case of Abbess Matilda of Essen and Aethelweard', *Early Medieval Europe*, 1 (1992), 53–68.

B. Yorke, 'The Bonifacian mission and female religious in Wessex', *Early Medieval Europe*, 7 (1998), 145–172.

D. Youngs, *The Life Cycle in Western Europe, c.1350–c.1500* (Manchester: Manchester UP, 2006).

Glossary

amanuensis	Scribe writing down the words of others
author	Creator of an original work
autograph	Made or written by the original author
excision	Cutting out or ignoring
genre	Classifying writing by style or purpose, e.g. drama, history, poetry
hagiographic	Relating to lives of saints
mediation	Any intervening process that distances the reader from the original author, and/or reshapes the work
orality	Based on the spoken or remembered, rather than the written
rubrics	Headings and subheadings to orient the reader, named for the red ink used for them in many manuscripts
topos	A recurrent theme or motif in writing, a standard element

6

Identities: Categories and Their Complications

'Identity politics'. This phrase is a useful way to describe how people sharing a certain characteristic or theoretical standpoint band together to campaign politically, whether for specific rights, or to overturn perceived and actual social injustices. We have already met identity politics in the discussion of early feminism and seen how contested that particular identity has become since the late nineteenth century. Feminist theory centres on social norms and expectations in three major areas: **production** (in terms of access to the rewards from economic activity, on which more presently), **reproduction** (in terms of control over one's own body and fertility, which we have discussed in Chapter 3) and **socialization** (briefly put, the ways in which children are brought up to mirror expectations of their parents and peers). In this chapter feminism is revisited as the impetus behind early histories of women, and we examine how it stimulated new attention to men's lives and masculinity in the Middle Ages, promoted not only by historians interested in gender issues, but others who *objected* to feminist politics intruding into their field. The section closes with a discussion of two more medieval authors, Margery Kempe and Christine de Pizan, who in different ways took on critics and left evidence of their agency.

The chapter then examines other political stances and identities that have fed into medieval gender history. Taking their cue from feminist historians and theorists challenging the 'invisibility' of women, mentioned in the previous chapter, scholars have actively sought – and continue to seek – evidence for the medieval lives of gay people (John Boswell's work, see Chapter 3), people of colour and people with physical or mental impairments. Not all share the characteristics of those they sought to study, but the common factor pushing for their inclusion in the historical narratives written now is the fact that, like women, these groups have organized and campaigned, or are still campaigning, to achieve political goals and rights for *their specific group*. This has had a profound effect on gender history, which has expanded to accommodate a broader spectrum of possibilities in its examination of the Middle Ages. History is also a powerful driver of social change, since it helps to illuminate, and disintegrate, arguments in favour of a particular state of affairs as 'natural' or 'it's always been this way'. We thus come full circle to the issue of taking the long view and connecting the medieval past with present concerns, with which we began.

Exceptional Women?

In the introduction I described feminist history as history concerned with women that was or could be used to expose and challenge social inequalities. What I might have added there was a note on the *collective* nature of feminist political action. Feminism sought – and still seeks – to change and improve the status of women through collaboration and **consciousness raising**. (We might note an early feminist history collection titled *Clio's Consciousness Raised*, published in 1974, for all that it skimmed over the medieval period.) Consciousness raising in the three areas of feminist theory might be achieved in any number of ways, and in early scholarship it often featured a focus on 'women overcoming' a particular obstacle, or 'transcending' their gender to take on roles more commonly occupied by men. For medieval historians, those obstacles were primarily the exclusion of women from political power. Thus we have numerous early biographies of queens and noblewomen who seemed to be 'exceptions' to this rule and, related, the incapacity of women to be warriors in a society geared for war (and again, 'exceptions' were soon found). Indeed, alongside Georgina Buckler's long-neglected biography of the Byzantine princess Anna Komnena, who featured in Chapter 5, there is a plethora of biographies of powerful medieval women, who came to prominence as queens, regents, heiresses or simply extraordinarily wealthy and visible in the sources. Some prominent women of the Middle Ages, such as Eleanor of Aquitaine, have several biographies devoted to them, such is their visibility and apparent power. Often, however, these biographies sought to position their subjects as in some way possessed of exceptional abilities that enabled them to transcend the expected roles of women in their era.

The 'biographical' approach was nothing new. Indeed biography has recently been described as 'the best attested narrative form of the Middle Ages' – bolstered, no doubt, by the literally hundreds of surviving medieval saints' lives (which are not, however, strictly biographical, being written largely to accepted norms of what a saint should be). Sanctity, of course, brought with it its own particular form of exceptionalism, whether in terms of resisting marriage (men and women), or performing feats of extreme self-denial (ditto), or writing and acting as a spiritual father/mother and guide to both women and men. Saints' lives, whether their subject was male or female, were written up to explore the possibilities of the religious life, but also to set firm parameters about what was and was not acceptable religious practice. Male saints' lives could be modelled on the life and miracles of Jesus; female saints might be portrayed establishing a relationship *with* Jesus. Many female saints' lives, however, feature the male confessor of the saint in an apparently secondary, but nevertheless authoritative role. The relationship between the two was highly gendered: although some abbesses gained sufficient authority to hear the confessions of their nuns, the monopoly of the male clergy on the rites of the Mass meant that the Church reinforced a gendered hierarchy of power.

The subjects of many saints' lives were female, but medieval biographies of secular people tended to focus on prominent men (Asser's life of Alfred the Great, for instance, or Michael Psellos' biographies of Byzantine emperors, modelled on earlier Roman templates). In the fourteenth century, however, the Italian author Giovanni Boccaccio wrote *On Famous Women* for Joanna I, queen of Naples (though eventually he included her as one of his subjects, and dedicated the work to the countess of Altavilla instead). Most of his figures were women from antiquity or myth, though the twelfth century figure of the Empress Constance (d. 1198) does appear as well. This was far from a work celebrating women *as* women, however. Boccaccio explicitly wrote his text as a commentary on good and bad behaviour, including the promise that he will be digressing with 'exhortations to virtue' along the way, and his preface included the comment that:

> If we grant that men deserve praise whenever they perform great deeds … how much more should women be extolled – almost all of whom are endowed by nature with soft, frail bodies and sluggish minds – when they take on a manly spirit show remarkable intelligence and bravery, and dare to execute deeds that would be extremely difficult even for men?

He also includes an openly misogynist story of Pope Joan. This story, based on earlier versions dating back to the thirteenth century, starts as a simple case of a young woman cross-dressing to achieve her aspirations to serve in the church, and ends in disaster as her female physiology (and obvious lack of chastity) result in her giving birth in the street as she participated as pope in a procession between the Lateran and the Colosseum. Boccaccio adds that as a result of this pollution (*spurcitia*) papal processions now avoided the 'detestable' site of her downfall. But the cross-dressing disguise at the heart of this particular story had been used to much more positive effect in stories of transvestite saints in the earlier church, particularly in the East. Disguising their bodily difference in monastic garb, and able, in this eastern context, to pass as male because their higher voices and beardlessness could be ascribed to eunuch status, several of these saints were only discovered to be female on their deaths, by which time their sanctity was undeniable.

Inspired by Boccaccio's work but responding to his misogyny and that of literary outputs closer to home, French author Christine de Pizan (d.c.1430), on whom more presently, wrote her *Book of the City of Ladies*, incorporating ancient and medieval women of power including the sixth century Frankish Queen Fredegund and the Empress Theodora, wife of the Byzantine Emperor Justinian I, and an array of female saints. This really was a celebration of women's capacities, and Christine's work found echoes in later scholarship. Elizabeth Elstob (1674–1752) planned an ambitious history of learned women such as herself, but her work was published under the name of her male collaborator, George Ballard, in 1752. Early in the following century, Mary Hays produced her six-volume *Female Biographies, or Memoirs of Illustrious and Celebrated Women* (London, 1803), with some 300 named figures that a modern collective of feminist scholars is now working to explore in greater depth. Biography is still an important part of consciousness raising, but current scholarship on female rulers emphasizes not their exceptionalism, but their ubiquity: look for aristocratic women wielding political power in the medieval period, and they are easily found. Tracing their family relationships, where visible, opens up a whole network of influential women, whether titled rulers or not. Their status *as women* was either not at issue at all, or mitigated by their wealth and rank: they simply ruled because they could.

But could they fight? This was of course the most masculine of medieval skills, and male children, particularly of the elite, were schooled early in martial skills through practice (often deadly dangerous, as reports of accidental deaths and woundings illustrate) and through related activities such as hunting. An early, and still rather rare, foray into the subject of medieval women warriors was made by Megan McLaughlin in 1990, and she framed her article in terms of their 'anomalous gender behaviour'. According to McLaughlin, before the eleventh century women engaging in warfare attracted little or no comment, whereas after that date the woman warrior was increasingly seen as 'unnatural'. McLaughlin's tentative frame was given more flesh by Carol Clover, who demonstrated how medieval Scandinavian texts present a society which accorded power not according to sex but according to behaviour, thus women took direct as well as indirect action, and men could be condemned for their passivity. Yet the transition from aristocratic household to emergent state structures in the twelfth century, McLaughlin argues, undermined the ability of aristocratic women, in particular, to perform duties in lieu of their husbands, including the defence of property by military means, what McLaughlin terms the 'domestic organization of warfare'. To a certain extent this article is influenced by Jo Ann McNamara's model of early medieval women's power through the family, and by the lurid stories of warlike and vengeful women (including Fredegund, for instance) related by early medieval authors such as Gregory of Tours. Reading the latter, it is no large leap to assume that early medieval women were Amazon-like creatures unfettered by male restrictions. In fact, early medieval laws had a real problem with women engaging in direct violence, as Ross Balzaretti has demonstrated for Italy and can also be noted in early Irish law.

Historians have subsequently challenged McLaughlin's closing-down of women's participation in military activities: David Hay's work on Countess Matilda of Tuscany (d. 1115) focused specifically on her active leadership of campaigns. Susan Edgington and Sarah Lambert co-edited a collection on gendering the crusading movement of the eleventh and twelfth centuries that went beyond documenting the camp followers so demonized by crusade preachers, and Helen Nicholson has written on the various roles that women played, noting that 'for most women, *as for most men*, the crusade was an expression of faith which they supported but in which they were not personally involved' [my emphasis]. Interest in elite women's role in defending and managing estates and castles in times of war and siege has demonstrated not only that such activities were possible, but also that they might form the basis of misogynist tales undermining them. The Norman author Orderic Vitalis' tale of the ignominious end to the siege of Breteuil castle, during which King Henry I's defiant daughter, Juliana, was forced to leap from the wall of the castle 'with bare buttocks' into the moat, is a case in point.

Measuring medieval women up as rulers and warriors, however, risks perpetuating the assumption that these are the things that 'matter' in medieval history, that the inclusion of gender in considerations of rulership and warfare is simply a matter of whether women 'did' these manly things or not. To a certain extent these questions are shaped by the concerns and language of medieval authors, which often referred to women as 'virile' or showing 'manliness' – the gender binary is at its most obvious here. Clearly, except in a very few isolated instances, a woman's desire to act in a manly way had its positive side, recognizing male superiority and aspiring to become male herself (those cross-dressing female saints come to mind again here). Yet there were boundaries to such ambitions: become *too* manly and a woman risked being attacked and condemned for her presumption, or marginalized as freakish in some way: Matilda's contemporary detractors focused on her 'unnatural' leadership of men, and Joan of Arc's execution as a heretic solved the problem of what to do with a young woman who had dressed in men's armour and led soldiers for the French king.

Medieval Feminist Identities? Christine de Pizan and Margery Kempe

Of course what Matilda and Joan's enemies were attacking was the apparently uncontrolled (by a man) agency of women and their supporters: both Matilda and Joan believed they were right to lead their campaigns, but their actions offered fuel to their critics. How then were women to respond? And did their voices seek to raise the consciousness of other women, even encourage them to collective action? What might 'feminism' represent in a medieval setting? Dhuoda's instructions to her son William could be read as contributing to his socialization, and thus as subversive in positioning her, rather than William's father, as the 'voice of authority' in their family, but this does not necessarily mean she was creating a model for other mothers to follow. Joan Kelly suggested that a feminist consciousness did exist in the Middle Ages, claiming that women such as Christine de Pizan, a prolific author whose writing provided a means of economic support after she was widowed (and thus connecting her directly with the rewards for her products), emphasized and challenged the patriarchal attitudes she encountered in a recognizably 'feminist' way, and that this continued as the late medieval and early modern 'Querelle des femmes [The debate about women]'.

Christine is often discussed alongside her close English contemporary, Margery Kempe, whom Verena Neuberger argued in 1994 was 'the first English feminist'. Margery and Christine had extremely contrasting lives, in fact their differing status challenges any attempt to privilege any one reason for their work having survived for us to read. Christine was the educated daughter of a courtier (specifically, the astrologer to the French king), whilst Margery was the illiterate daughter of the mayor of Lynn, in Norfolk, and wife of a merchant. Both women were married, though Christine was widowed early with three small children. Margery had fourteen pregnancies, although we do not know how many of her offspring survived. The texts produced by both were written in their respective vernacular languages, rather than Latin, and they were almost exact contemporaries, living until their sixties and born within a decade of each other in the latter half of the fourteenth century.

Both Margery and Christine have attracted a disproportionate amount of attention from historians of women and gender. Both their lives challenged accepted norms: Christine had to write to support herself and her family, and did not remarry, as might have been expected of a young widow. Margery claimed to have visions of Christ from an early age, which eventually led to her renouncing her life as a wife, mother and none-too-successful entrepreneur (she had engaged in brewing, her failure at which she attributed to God's anger at her excessive pride) to go on pilgrimage to Jerusalem and dictate her autobiography and mystical visions to successive scribes. Thus both women's lives were characterized by a claimed autonomy from male control, challenging the patriarchal expectation that they should remain subject to male authority. Both regained control over their reproductive lives, and both were also, more or less, economically independent, and this gave them choices that many women in the later Middle Ages (or earlier, for that matter) just would not have had.

Secondly, Christine in particular challenged prevailing misogynist language in the writings of her male contemporaries (catalysed by the earlier *Roman de la Rose* of Jean de Meun) and responded with the *Book of the City of Ladies*, published in 1405, that celebrated the achievements of notable women. Neither she nor Margery, however, was writing biography in its strict sense of a life recounted: the women in their texts were designed to offer models or *exempla*, a moral to the story that the reader could identify with. The success of the *Book of the City of Ladies* can be measured perhaps by the fact that it was published in an English translation in the sixteenth century. Christine's use of historical examples might certainly be interpreted as consciousness raising of sorts, transmitting the achievements of earlier women to inspire present change. But she went still further: her *Treasure of the City of Ladies/Book of the Three Virtues*, argued for more widespread girls' education. Christine had used her own education to enable her to gain a measure of economic independence, and so campaigning for more girls' education potentially opened up this route for others to follow. It is little wonder, therefore, that she is celebrated as an example of medieval feminist writing.

Margery's *Book* was both more ambitious, in seeking to detail both her life and express the visions she had experienced, but more limited in scope in that the only woman it seeks to defend is Margery herself. She freely admits that her behaviour frequently upset and antagonized people, both strangers and neighbours, and whilst she claimed her actions were sanctioned by Christ himself, she may not have been seen as a desirable role model of female emancipation from family concerns. Yet she tells us she had visited the anchoress and mystic Julian of Norwich for advice: Liz Herbert McAvoy has read this visit as a quest to 'evade the proscriptions of the **phallic** script', i.e. to find a feminine space and a female mentor to help her in her spiritual journey. Again, whether Margery saw it this way is open to interpretation.

So did these texts function as a consciousness raising exercises? Whilst Christine lived, she herself worked hard on having copies of her work produced and circulated, but they were, after all, literary works, accessible only to a literate elite. Margery's autobiography seems not to have enjoyed a wide readership, and in fact the complete text only resurfaced in the 1930s. So is it at all helpful to ask whether these two women were feminists? In asking this question, we need to remember that the term 'feminist' was itself a **neologism** of the nineteenth century, coined to express the hopes and aspirations of the first wave campaigners for women's rights. It goes without saying, therefore, that neither Christine de Pizan and Margery Kempe would have been termed 'feminist' in the fifteenth century, nor would they have identified themselves as such. Yet historians such as Roberta Krueger still see Christine as the starting point of a move 'towards feminism'. Should we therefore even look for 'feminism' in the medieval period? Simply put, no, but feminism's triple themes of economic, reproductive and educational rights enables us to pose interesting questions about how medieval society viewed these issues. It allows Helen Jewell, for example, to ask whether Geoffrey Chaucer's *Wife of Bath* is simply misogynist, or whether in fact it was written to subvert misogynist views.

It is tempting to think of medieval women like Christine and Margery sharing the same feelings as their modern counterparts, the one trying to challenge established norms with her writing, the other seeking a more fulfilling life outside of home and family, and thus to label them as feminists. Feminist readings also interpret the actions of Margery and other female visionaries as claims to autonomy and authority. It has often been suggested that, denied a position of real authority in the Church, particularly after the reform movement of the eleventh century, women increasingly developed an interior religious life that focused heavily on their personal devotion to Christ (or Mary, or the Host) and expressed itself in often quite visceral and bodily visions, centring on a direct spiritual and emotional bond. Such experiences, as Margery found, might excite suspicion and accusations of heresy, or might be interpreted as a sign of sanctity and holiness.

So much for individual feminisms, what about collective action? Natalie Zemon Davies, in her 1976 article (see Chapter 2), highlighted the limitations of documenting individual women and the ways in which biographies formed simply a starting point to an investigation into the processes of women's power and agency. Her call for more nuanced work found responses from historians in the United States and United Kingdom, and there was a shift from the individual to collective, and to a study of the ideologies that underpinned active women's positions. Alongside individual queens, therefore, queenship as an institution was explored, and continues to provide a rich theme for discussion. Pauline Stafford, whilst writing on prominent women of Anglo-Saxon England (see Chapter 2), sought to explore the *dynamics* of power relations through women's life-cycle events, rather than simply trace their lives. Stafford's multiple studies on female agency in Anglo-Saxon England set influential precedents, whilst for medieval Francia Jinty Nelson provided equally subtle – indeed parallel – studies of queenship and familial relations in the Merovingian and Carolingian courts. Both scholars brought keen, feminist eyes to their material, and together with their colleague Régine Le Jan (see Appendix) arguably helped to shape the transition from 'women' to 'gender' in early medieval history-writing.

Given the fact that religious women formed communities with and without official sanction, did this represent another form of feminist collectivity? Or was the highly personal nature of religious devotion an obstacle to its use as a tool for self-determination? I highlighted above the idea of fourth wave as a fragmented, issue-based form of feminist politics, and this might be a better way of viewing the individual case studies that have attracted attention in the medieval evidence. When groups of women joined forces in the Middle Ages – and the cases we have are quite rare, since they needed to be worthy of record – they often did so to address a specific problem, not to improve the global status of women. Katherine French has highlighted the case of Johanna Moreland in the late medieval records from Westminster. Johanna used her female networks in this close-knit community to raise money to build a new parish church in the fifteenth century. Viewed through a fourth- rather than a second-wave feminist lens, this is 'feminism', utilizing accepted forms of female activity (in this case, piety combined with charitable intent) to benefit her community, but also to enhance her own **social capital**.

Economic Status, Class Identities and Power

Examining the cases of Margery Kempe and Christine de Pizan usefully reminds us that true agency often depends on access to independent economic resources. Access to the proceeds of work in fact lay at the heart of early feminist studies of medieval women. These cross-cut with Marxist studies of the detrimental effects of industrialization, which removed work from the domestic space and into factories, and thus divorced the worker from the direct benefits of her or his labour. We have already noted the London School of Economics as an early and hospitable centre for feminist scholarship. Annie Abram, herself an LSE product, published her doctoral thesis as *Social England in the Fifteenth Century* in 1909, and then wrote on female traders in later medieval London for the *Economic Journal* in 1916. The essays of Eileen Power (Professor of Economic History at LSE from 1931) and Marion K. Dale, originally published in the 1930s, were reprinted in the 1970s and 1980s when women's equal pay was at the forefront of political debate and feminist historians, particularly Judith Bennett (on whose work more presently), were beginning to recognize that they were not the first to notice the enduring pay gap between men's and women's work. The latter decades of the twentieth century recognized Power and Dale as pioneers in the field of women's history, although as Maxine Berg has pointed out in Power's case, her profile and memory diminished as the career of her husband, M. M. Postan, took off and overshadowed the work she had done alone and in collaboration with him.

In contrast to the biographical approach taken by her contemporaries, Power focused on the contrast between ideals set up by normative sources such as laws from Church and state, and the reality of most medieval women's lives. Power's model was of 'pit and pedestal' – the contrast between the religious model of women as inheritors of Eve's transgression, and later literary portrayals of women as distant love objects; but her own background in economics and use of non-narrative sources led her to the conclusion that overall medieval women enjoyed a 'rough and ready equality' with men (implicitly, within the same social *class*) which they subsequently lost. Unusually, therefore, she was holding up the medieval period as one to be celebrated, rather than used as a (low) starting point for the progressive improvement of women's rights. Her assessment of women's status perhaps seems a little optimistic in the light of more recent studies that reveal unwritten power relations, but at the time she was not alone in her view. Written just after Power's essay, Marian Dale's consideration of the London silk women, again drawing on fiscal records, suggests a sense of dissatisfaction with normative texts, and a desire to bring more detailed and nuanced studies to bear on the question of status. Hers is also a history interested in the collective, rather than the individual, albeit a collective that worked in a luxury industry.

The history of production focused on women's work, within and outside the home, and confronted not only the fact that women's paid work tended to be lower paid than men's (still a live issue), but also women's 'double burden' of taking care of home and children alongside any paid work. We saw in the discussion of legal norms above how the mythology of women's place in the home was used as a means for justifying her subjection to her wage-earning husband, and how this model, largely a product of **proto-industrialization**, neglected to take into account the fact that most women needed to earn as well in most households.

Second-wave feminists, too, sought to trace the origins of women's economic oppression and resistance in earlier history, rediscovering these early studies on the way. Again, some took a more optimistic view than others. In 1989, for example, Caroline Barron revisited the question of Power's 'equality' in an article that has become the cornerstone of a lively debate, 'The "Golden Age" of women in medieval London'. Judith Bennett, on the other hand, has argued that apparent moments of economic and/or social advances for women were and are rapidly counteracted by other constrictions on their agency, restoring what she has termed the **patriarchal equilibrium**. Her own work on later medieval England, in particular her study of female brewers, highlighted how men's generally superior access to economic resources eventually enabled the transformation of that industry from a domestic undertaking that could be fitted around other tasks, to one requiring expensive equipment and/or new raw materials, squeezing women out. Because men enjoyed access to social networks that were off limits to (respectable) women, and formalized that sociability through craft guilds and professional associations, they were able to pool resources for expensive investments in brewing equipment. A similar story is visible in the textile industry, Dale's silk women excepted, and both Jeremy Goldberg and Barbara Hanawalt have reflected on women's marginalization within production, albeit from differing viewpoints.

It is no coincidence that all of these historians chose to work on the relatively dense evidence of later medieval England, and were contributing and responding to debates about the negative effects of the Industrial Revolution on women's (and men's) working lives. But just as we have seen that 'feminist consciousness' is largely in the eye of the modern beholder, so class consciousness, too, is a vexed question in medieval studies. Peasants' revolts (such as those in England, often now termed the 'Great Rising', or that of the Ciompi in Florence) and other 'popular' movements turn out often to have been sparked off not by a sense of class solidarity, but specific issues that led to violent protest. At their heart was often a sense of disempowerment, and this raises the question of how gender historians might re-examine such movements. Beyond documenting the minority of women within these protests (and their aftermaths), a gendered analysis can also explore the loss of masculine identity that drove men to rebel. Derek Neal has touched briefly upon this issue for the English revolt, and Samuel Cohn for the Florentine uprising.

Being a Man: Masculinity and Identity

Early feminist history-writing that sought to prove women's equality to men in all sectors fell into the trap of using existing masculine frameworks and trying to fit women into them – the 'add women and stir' approach.

Yet feminist history also encountered a serious backlash from the early 1980s onwards. Allen Frantzen's essay 'When women aren't enough', published in 1993, whilst ostensibly framed as a discussion of how gender studies that included men had emerged, contained such comments as 'Feminism required merely that everybody talk about women, which, it seems, everybody was willing to do, in particular a host of guilty men eager to be identified with an undeniably powerful trend.' Setting up this parodic picture that effectively delegitimized 'talking about women', and Frantzen's opening comment in the same article about being the 'token man' in the *Speculum* special issue in which this piece appeared, not only misrepresented feminism, but also, coming from an authoritative voice in medieval studies, legitimized further attacks that have continued into the new millennium. For example, the 'omnipresent feminist code of ethics, which tends to conceive of women only in the role of victims', is blamed by Nira Gradowicz-Pancer for *closing off* discussions of women as perpetrators of violence in the early medieval period. Following on from the breathtaking inaccuracy of this statement, Gradowicz-Pancer suggests that 'entering into a debate ... would not be relevant here'. Of *course* we should enter into a debate, particularly when a colleague feels it necessary to distort, and distance herself from, feminist medieval history. Like it or not, it is much more common to find women recorded as victims of violence in medieval texts than as perpetrators, and that is because of how medieval authors understand female roles, not a feminist 'code'.

For some feminists, however, gender represented a direct threat to the ground they had gained (unsurprising, given Frantzen's explicit positioning), not just because it offered a 'back door' to restore male hegemony through the study of masculinity (on which more presently), but also because of its inherently negotiable nature. Judith Bennett argued – in the third issue of *Gender and History* itself – that it diverted attention from the explicitly feminist goals of women's history. She has maintained this stance in her book length re-evaluation of the field in 2006 (see Chapter 1), arguing that gender history has shifted the focus away from 'concrete, accessible histories and towards analyses that can be abstract in both subject matter and exposition'. Legal historian Joan Hoff agreed, and took issue in 1994 with the ways in which gender theorists destabilized the possibility of reconstructing past social realities. One issue that particularly exercised her was the fact that this theoretical approach might distance scholars in the US, who had embraced it, from their colleagues elsewhere in the world, who maintained a more **empirical** outlook. (In this she was prescient.) She also argued that using gender eliminated the category of women, and in doing so represented a patriarchal approach, imposing a new orthodoxy that denied the possibility of historical truth and thus undermining feminist scholarship that had used past histories in political campaigns in the present.

This tension was explored by Judith Butler's text, *Gender Trouble*, which has been extensively cited by historians and literary scholars since its publication in 1990. Explicitly confronting the concerns of feminists that 'the indeterminacy of gender might eventually culminate in the failure of feminism', Butler explored how gender categories that supported hierarchy and privileged heterosexual relations over all others needed the work of critics to expose the ways in which 'women' had been defined in relation to norms and assumptions, and with a language gendered and centred on the male. Troubling these assumptions lay at the heart of her work and that of the philosophers she cites – Foucault above all (whom she nevertheless criticizes for his indifference to gender in his work on sexuality), but also Mary Douglas. For Butler, therefore, the work of gender studies was to *resist* 'domestication', to challenge hierarchical assumptions and to maintain a feminist agenda encompassing attention to the marginal. What is striking is how much of this debate was essentially centred on North American academic concerns: it did not prevent other scholars from continuing to examine women's lives, but it did, as Hoff suggested, threaten to marginalize a substantial proportion of the academy. A German translation of *Gender Trouble* was published in 1991, but it was not translated into French or Italian until 2006.

One, none too subtle, response to the emergence of feminist-sponsored women's studies curricula, and the opening up of gender studies as an alternative route, was the establishment of men's studies as an area of research, a phenomenon trackable to the 1980s in the US. As politicized as feminist movements, men's groups then and now cover a vast spectrum of stances, some virulently misogynist (Frantzen's current work outside academia belongs in this category), others seeing gender theory as an important tool for analysing men's lives in the past, and as a way of exploring male-female relations and developing critical work on the subject of masculinity, which allows for a greater range of identities that are not only associated with men. How did this trend manifest itself in medieval history?

Superficially, masculinity proved a rich field for medievalists to excavate. We have already examined the physiological aspects and regulatory frameworks surrounding being a man. Whilst the feminist themes of production, reproduction and socialization had been primarily theorized to examine women's lives, their utility – particularly the question of socialization – for examining men was obvious: what did medieval mothers (and fathers) *expect* their sons and daughters to do? What were they expected to pass on as parental guidance? Our answer comes partly in the laws, penitentials and conduct books we met in Chapter 4, setting down the 'rules'. But the much greater visibility of men in medieval texts means we can delve more deeply into the assumptions that worked to shape masculine identity.

The sources are not primarily concerned to reflect on what it meant to *be* a man, and to behave in an acceptably masculine way, but they are often quick to condemn behaviour that risked making a man look 'womanish'. Furthermore, the influence of the mother on her son's development had to be interrupted if he was not to grow up to be 'girly' (socialization being at the heart of a mother's role). This separation process, which for the sons of the medieval elite often manifested itself in being placed in a male relative's household, it is suggested, meant that learning to be masculine was fraught with anxiety. Boyhood, whilst not entirely free of constraints, gave way to a social adulthood where gender categories became set. Conserving femininity, for girls, by contrast, was largely structured as a passive process, learning what *not* to do rather than striving to outshine others as boys were encouraged to do. Cordelia Beattie argues that, unlike masculinity, 'femininity was never contested, sought or paraded in the way that masculinity was (however defined)'. She encompasses in this statement the qualitative difference, in terms of how prized each was, between being masculine and being feminine.

The clues needed to be worked out, text by text, and the initial, rather simplistic approach was to focus not on what men *were* but what they *did* – warriors, clergy, monks, kings, peasants. This, however, immediately had the welcome but largely unintended effect of turning 'masculinity' into 'masculinities' – just as feminist studies had realized and acknowledged that not all women's experiences could be treated as universals, so with the benefit of that knowledge feminist work on masculinity did not seek to define a one-size 'masculinity' that fit all. A volume of essays published in 1994 on *Medieval Masculinities* demonstrated that the editors were conscious of the **plurality** of male identities and did not assume that all men had similar experiences. What then made a medieval man 'masculine'? The essays in the 1994 collection in which McNamara's *Herrenfrage* essay appeared (see above, Chapter 3) focus on biological/medical understandings of maleness, the image of the hero in literature, husbands and fathers, male monks and images of masculinity in Jewish and Muslim culture, viewed from a Christian perspective. A 1999 collection gathered historical and archaeological evidence, and asked not only about representations of masculinity but also its formation from early boyhood. Janet Nelson's essay in this volume, for example, reflects on how the expectations of elite families may have caused some boys difficulties in embracing their duties and position.

Gender historians continue to be heavily influenced by Judith Butler's idea that gender roles have constantly to be 'performed' in order to maintain and reinforce them. This formulation was a gift for those working on medieval masculinity, for the sources often tell us much more about what men *did* than about their interior lives. Indeed, such was the attractiveness of this element of Butler's work that it has often been used to bolster quite traditional views of male activity in the Middle Ages, ignoring both her feminist stance and the fact of negotiation at the heart of performance. Every action – whether of martial prowess, physical labour, piety, leadership, husbanding, fathering children, engaging in property transactions, or rebellion – was temporary, contingent, more often than not witnessed by others who would remember and relate what they had seen, but requiring repetition and constant reinforcement. So boys and men had to be and *act* like boys and men all the time even if they didn't much *feel* like doing so.

Gender as performance needs to be carefully defined, however, if we are not to fall into the trap of thinking that performativity is always associated with visible actions – performing passivity (whether in deference to other males, or, in the case of girls, because they were expected to be passive) takes practice and perhaps even more self-control. The now well-established approach of considering and tracking evidence of medieval emotions, epitomized by the work of Barbara Rosenwein and of researchers at the Australian Centre for the History of the Emotions at Adelaide, has perhaps been more successful in assessing how different emotions were expressed, recorded and deployed by the literate elite to make moralizing statements, rather than how they were actually experienced. It is striking, for instance, that all of the case studies in a volume *Anger's Past* dealt with male subjects.

Young men had to strive to achieve the social status of their elders, in whose interests it might have been to keep their younger counterparts in a state of perpetual youth. Jeremy Goldberg has tracked this phenomenon in later medieval English court records detailing disobedient and unruly apprentices, whilst in Italy scholars have traced the phenomenon of public, and often highly ritualized, fights between gangs of youths. Both groups it is clear were kicking against the norms that their youth and subjection to other males imposed upon them. This tension between men for hegemony (a concept, as we have seen, influenced by R. W. Connell's work, see Chapter 4) is expressed in the title of two other volumes of essays from the 1990s, *Becoming Male in the Middle Ages* and *Conflicted Identities and Multiple Masculinities*. Here a diverse range of work revisited themes already becoming canonical – sexuality and celibacy, husbands, military prowess – but introduced considerations of castration, fluid gender identity in literature, and in the latter case called for medievalists to 'continue to examine the intersection of competing and contradictory masculinities that uneasily co-existed in medieval society'. These contradictory masculinities, according to Jeffrey Jerome Cohen and Bonnie Wheeler, editors of *Becoming Male*, were due to the fact that 'gender, like time and space, is continually negotiated' (here they exhibit the influence of Butler's work), and for that reason they refused, in their introduction, to offer any definition of '"masculinity", "masculinities" or even "medieval masculinities"'. It is striking how work on medieval masculinities appeared in print in this fragmented, essay-based way, as if addressing the issue in its entirety in a book-length study represented too much of a challenge for any single scholar until Ruth Mazo Karras's first foray in 2002 (see Chapter 4).

How did the theme of medieval masculinity/masculinities fare after these first efforts to capture its myriad forms? One of the most interesting developments has been the way in which the early emphasis on 'becoming' masculine has been replaced, or at least supplemented, by studies on how masculinity might be threatened or lost. We have already noted responses to male infertility and impotency. Physical impairment could prevent a man being a full man, if his role (as warrior, cultivator, or artisan) was compromised by the injury. Appearance has also formed the focus of several studies, with subjects ranging from men's fashions to cross-dressing, or to hair and its loss, particularly facial hair. All of these topics draw upon existing paradigms of women's history, but offer new insight into what it was *like* to be a man.

But has 'masculinity' had its moment? In a volume that was published in 2011, John Tosh, one of the pioneers of masculinity studies in history (his 1994 essay 'What should historians do with masculinity?', though focused on the nineteenth century, is regularly cited by scholars working on other periods), asked instead whether the history of masculinity was now an outdated concept. It has allowed many scholars who did not self-identify as gender historians to write on the topic, and a considerable amount of literature emerged uncritically examining how images of masculinity were invariably constructed as the polar opposite of femininity. Ultimately, the unease over masculinity seems to lie in misinterpretations that maintain a stark binary opposition – what is masculine is not feminine, and vice versa – that did not adequately express the spectrum of gender possibilities that Butler and her followers envisaged. Crucially, in some cases this served not only to reinforce existing approaches to medieval history (in particular providing new energy to topics such as rulership and warfare, without necessarily introducing new insights), but also underplayed the plurality of masculine models open to analysis in medieval Europe. Gilbert Herdt's *Third Sex, Third Gender*, published in 1994, had already proposed a range of identities with only loose connections to 'male' and 'female' bodies as traditionally understood. For Herdt, the fluidity of gender identity meant that the old binary of male-female was no longer fit for purpose in critical analysis.

Religious and Ethnic Identities: Beyond 'Other'

McNamara's complementary theses of a change in status for both men *and* women in the eleventh and twelfth centuries, and the scholarship that has followed or challenged her models, share a significant flaw in that they focus almost entirely on the Christian majority in medieval Europe, and do not explore how far (if at all) the apparent shift in gendered relations works if we look instead at religious and ethnic minorities such as the Jewish community, Muslim cultures and people of colour in medieval Europe.

To take one example, we saw in Chapter 4 that Simha Goldin argues for an *improvement* in the status of Jewish women in the twelfth century, as Jews came under increasing external attack and drew strength from the rituals surrounding family and home, many of which were led by women. Male community leaders, however, whilst still secure in their religious status, were often unable to protect their communities from crippling economic demands or worse, devastating pogroms such as those in Granada in 1066 (at the hands of Muslims), the Rhineland in 1096 (by Christian 'crusaders'), York in 1190 (where the local perpetrators were clearly known to their victims) and so on. Goldin himself has studied medieval Jewish martyrdom, focusing particularly on the phenomenon of Jewish husbands sacrificing their wives and children in preference to having them killed or forcibly converted by their enemies. Masculinity in this context is not about martial prowess, but defending the faith with extreme measures. Faced with such resistance, attacks on Jewish masculinity took other forms, directed at Jewish male bodies. Christian **polemicists** of the thirteenth century suggested that Jewish men menstruated like women, an idea that combined the almost universal repugnance surrounding menstrual bleeding with the perceived passivity of Jewish men that effeminized them in Christian eyes.

Medievalists have begun to use modern, postcolonial theory as a means of understanding not only the medieval past, but how its historiography has been subtly (and not so subtly) shaped by models of Eurocentric imperialism. A key tool of appropriation of other cultures was the translation of the literature into the language of the dominant majority, and then using such translations to attack and stigmatize the religious or cultural practices of those cultures, or at the very least to misrepresent them to suit political or religious goals. This was precisely what happened in the staged Jewish-Christian debates of the thirteenth and fourteenth centuries. How far back does this colonial voice extend? There is still some way to go to entirely remove the whiff of the exotic, oriental Other from some historical studies of still central topics such as the European crusades to the East, and increasing pressures on non-Christian peoples within Europe's boundaries.

But what is this 'Other'? Here we meet another philosophical and theoretical tool that has had enormous influence within medieval studies. Based on German philosopher Georg Hegel's model of the Self needing an Other against which to define itself, the term was picked up in French thought of the twentieth century as a psychoanalytic tool enabling a radical, and usually opposite, counterpart to the Self. The tool of definition, in all cases, was language – the description of the Other was **constitutive**, and gender historians picked up on the ways in which the masculine Self wrote women as Other, Not-Men, Not-Us. Even the tendency in modern historiography of the Middle Ages to discuss 'women saints' or 'women writers' is a direct legacy of an academic world that regarded male saints and writers as the norm.

But otherness (or Otherness) could relate to particular groups and communities as well, and this is where the growing use of the term has reinforced some prevailing tendencies within medieval history to see the western, Christian community voice as the norm, a standard against which groups and individuals were judged. The Anglo-Norman colonization of parts of Ireland, Wales and southern Europe gave rise to descriptions of the subjected people in gendered terms: as sexually deviant, with male leaders emasculated by their defeat. As European Christendom expanded in the twelfth and thirteenth centuries, more texts were written (often inspired in fact by Muslim geographies) that sought to describe journeys, real and imagined, and to map the known world. Scholars such as Sharon Kinoshita have opened up the potential of gendered and postcolonial readings of this material, and several volumes of largely literary studies have now been published. The relative neglect from historians may belie the inherently crafted nature of such texts and the difficulty – perceived or real – of extracting from them any semblance of historical data. Whilst this argument may hold for the more fantastically fictional and creative outputs of medieval literature, it does not account for the relative neglect of the rich, cultural descriptions contained in works by clerics, geographers, pilgrims, ambassadors and merchants that still tend to be used selectively for their most outrageous or spectacular vignettes of prejudice against non-Europeans, emphasizing their **alterity**. We are now far from trying to reconstruct 'how it really was' in history, and open to exploring the influences and experiences that the writers were trying to convey. What is particularly worthy of note, perhaps, is the way in which women, and the treatment of women, figure in these descriptions as a measure of how 'civilized' (or not) such peoples were, as Kim Phillips has recently highlighted. The value lies not so much in whether these were accurate portrayals as in how such accounts reflect the norms and assumptions of the mainly male writers themselves.

Postcolonial readings of medieval travel literature would start from the perspective of those being observed and commented about by western writers. Thus in the case of a young male traveller such as Marco Polo, whose account of his travels in the East is peppered with hints as to how he enjoyed some recreational time with the exotic foreign women he encountered, we would be examining rather more critically his casual 'use' of such sexual partners and perhaps drawing uncomfortable comparisons with more recent sexual exploitation of 'native' women in modern, colonized countries. The objectification of women also features in clerical texts of writers and missionaries in the thirteenth and fourteenth centuries again, this and other similar material focusing in on either the extreme beauty – or more often on the extreme strangeness – of local womenfolk in the East demands to be re-examined not as colourful prose, but as the misogynist and racist stereotyping it actually is.

Race provides a significant challenge to medieval historians of gender relations, not least because it is still debated whether medieval identities were formulated in racialized terms corresponding with modern understandings. The explicitly racialized language of some thirteenth century university texts emanating from Paris, for example, may or may not represent broader social realities. Cross-cultural work is still relatively rare in medieval studies, but it is notable that 'ethnicity' has been preferred to 'race' as a term to indicate difference between groups, and when medieval

Europeans did meet other peoples, their starting point in describing them often referred to religious practices alongside physical difference. Elisheva Baumgarten's exploration of childbirth rituals is a good example of this (see Chapter 3), combining the experiences of Christian and Jewish communities and, crucially, examining the role of men alongside women in the first few months of a child's life.

The problem with Otherness as a category is that it has come to represent an unproblematic blanket term for those in the minority or on the margins of medieval society, that is, it assumes that the Self here is the male, clerical, white, able-bodied medieval writer whose description of such groups is authoritative for our picture of medieval society and culture. This is of course partly a product of the skew in the sources: we don't have many first-person accounts of what it was like to be poor, or sick, or stigmatized in some way. Such people appear mainly in hagiographic texts as recipients of cures – or, increasingly from the thirteenth century, religious conversion – which again reinforces the idea that there was a 'norm' which had to be adhered to. But this is only one side of the story. How can gender historians use such normative texts yet excavate the viewpoint of the silent object of such descriptions? In my own work on disfigurement, I have found that victims not only sought solace in prayer (a passive response), but turned their apparent misfortune into a didactic tool – a blinded man receiving alms, for example, offered a lesson in Christian (or Jewish, or Muslim) charity, patience and humility. At least one victim of severe disfigurement, we are told, exhibited his still attached but displaced eyeball for money. This sits rather uncomfortably with the idea that people with disabilities were passive recipients of help, and suggests that if we pay closer attention to our texts, the apparent silence of subaltern groups is anything but total.

Source Hunt: Individual and Group Identities

To what extent can we find identity labels in medieval texts, and what do they tell us about how people categorized themselves and others? What stereotypes can you find?

Sources

A. Blamires, *Woman Defamed and Woman Defended* (Oxford: Oxford University Press, 1992).

The Book of Margery Kempe, tr. B. A. Windeatt (London: Penguin, 1985).

Christine de Pizan, *The Book of the City of Ladies*, tr. R. Brown-Grant (London: Penguin, 2004).

Christine de Pizan, *The Treasure of the City of Ladies*, or, *The Book of the Three Virtues*, tr. S. Lawson (London: Penguin, 2003).

Ibn Battuta, *The Travels of Ibn Battuta*, tr. H. Gibb and C. F. Beckingham, abridged version with introduction by T. Broadhurst-Smith (London: Picador, 2003).

Ibn Fadlan and the Land of Darkness: Arab Travellers in the Far North, tr. C. Stone and P. Lund (London: Penguin, 2011).

Ibn Jubayr, *The Travels of Ibn Jubayr*, tr. R. J. C. Broadhurst (London: Cape, 1952).

John Mandeville, *The Travels of Sir John Mandeville*, tr. C. Moseley (London: Penguin, 2005).

Jewish Travellers in the Middle Ages: 19 Firsthand Accounts, ed. and tr. Elkan N. Adler (New York: Dover, 1987 [1930]).

Marco Polo, *The Travels of Marco Polo*, tr. B. Colbert (London: Wordsworth, 1997).

Key Reading

J. Bennett, 'Feminism and history', *Gender and History*, 1 (1989), 251–271.

J. Bennett, 'Review essay: 'History that stands still': women's work in the European past', *Feminist Studies* 14 (1988), 269–283.

J. Butler, 'Performative acts and gender constitution', *Theatre Journal*, 40 (1988), 519–531.

M. K. Dale, 'The London silk women of the 15th century', *Economic History Review*, 1st series, 4 (1933), reprinted with preceding commentary by M. Kowaleski and J. Bennett, 'Crafts, guilds and women in the Middle Ages: fifty years after Marian K. Dale', in J. Bennett et al., eds, *Sisters and Workers in the Middle Ages* (Chicago, IL: Chicago University Press, 1989).

B. Gottlieb, 'The problem of feminism in the 15th century', in J. Kirshner and S. Wemple, eds, *Women of the Medieval World* (Oxford: Blackwell, 1985).

G. Heng, 'The invention of race in the European middle ages', *Literature Review*, 8 (2011), 315–350.

J. Hoff, 'Gender as a postmodern category of paralysis', *Women's History Review*, 3.2 (1994), 149–168.

J. Kelly, 'The social relations of the sexes: methodological implications of women's history', *Signs*, 1 (1976), 809–823.

J. Kelly, 'Early Feminist Theory and the *Querelle des Femmes*, 1400–1789', *Signs*, 8 (1982), reprinted in fuller version in her *Women History and Theory* (Chicago, IL: Chicago University Press, 1984).

R. Krueger, 'Towards feminism: Christine de Pisan, female advocacy, and women's textual communities in the late middle ages and beyond', in *The Oxford Handbook of Women and Gender in Medieval Europe*, ed. J. M. Bennett and R. Mazo Karras (Oxford, 2013), 590–606.

M. McLaughlin, 'The woman warrior: gender, warfare and society in medieval Europe', *Women's Studies*, 17 (1990): 193–209.

E. Power, *Medieval Women* (Cambridge: Cambridge University Press, 1975).

E. Power, 'The position of women in the middle ages', in C. G. Crump and E. F. Jacob, eds, *The Legacy of the Middle Ages* (1926).

J. Tosh, 'What should historians do with masculinity?' *History Workshop*, 38 (1994), 179–202.

J. Tosh, 'The history of masculinity: an outdated concept?' in *What is Masculinity?* ed. J. A. Arnold and S. Brady (London: Palgrave Macmillan, 2011), 17–34.

Further Reading

A. Abram, 'Women traders of medieval London', *Economic Journal*, 26 (1916), 276–285.

Ross Balzaretti, '"These are things that men do, not women': The Social Regulation of Female Violence in Langobard Italy," in Guy Halsall, ed., *Violence and Society in the Early Medieval West* (Woodbridge: Boydell, 1998), 175–92.

C. Barron, 'The "Golden Age" of women in medieval London', *Reading Medieval Studies*, 15 (1989), 35–58.

C. Beattie, 'Gender and femininity in medieval England', in N. Partner, ed., *Writing Medieval History* (London: Hodder Arnold, 2005), 153–170.

Becoming Male in the Middle Ages, ed. J. J. Cohen and B. Wheeler (New York: Routledge, 2000).

M. Berg, *A Woman in History: Eileen Power, 1889–1940* (Cambridge: Cambridge University Press, 1996).

R. Blumenfeld-Kosinski, 'Christine de Pizan and the misogynistic tradition', *Romanic Review*, 81 (1990).

G. Bock, 'Women's history and gender history: aspects of an international debate', *Gender and History*, 1 (1989), 7–30.

R. Brown-Grant, *Christine de Pizan and the Moral Defence of Women: Reading Beyond Gender* (Cambridge: Cambridge University Press, 1999).

J. Butler, *Gender Trouble: Feminism and the Subversion of Identity* (New York: Routledge, 1990).

M. Caviness, 'Feminism, gender studies and medieval studies', *Diogenes*, 57 (2010), 30–45.

C. Clover, 'Regardless of sex: men, women and power in early Northern Europe', *Representations*, 44 (1993): 1–28.

S. K. Cohn, 'Repression of popular revolt in late medieval and early renaissance Italy', in S. K. Cohn and F. Ricciardelli, eds, *The Culture of Violence in Renaissance Italy* (Florence: Le Lettere, 2012), 99–122.

S. K. Cohn, 'Women in revolt in late medieval and early modern Europe', in J. Firnhaber-Baker and D. Schonaers, eds, *The Routledge History Handbook of Medieval Revolt* (Abingdon: Routledge, 2017), 208–219.

L. Collingridge, '"Please don't talk about Hildegard and feminism in the same breath!"' *Medieval Feminist Forum*, 34 (2002), 35–43.

Conflicted Identities and Multiple Masculinities: Men in the Medieval West, ed. J. Murray (New York: Routledge, 1999).

L. Crompton, 'The myth of lesbian impunity: capital laws from 1270–1791', *Journal of Homosexuality*, 6 (1980/1), 11–25.

K. French, 'Well-behaved women can make history: women's friendships in late medieval Westminster', in *Writing Medieval Women's Lives*, ed. C. Newman Goldy and A. Livingstone (New York: Palgrave Macmillan, 2012), 247–266.

Gendering the Crusades, ed. S. B. Edgington and S. Lambert (Cardiff: University of Wales Press, 2001).

P. J. P. Goldberg, 'Migration, youth and gender in later medieval England', in P. J. P. Goldberg and F. Riddy, ed., *Youth in the Middle Ages* (Woodbridge: Boydell, 2004), 85–99.

N. Gradowicz-Pancer, 'De-gendering female violence: Merovingian female honour as an "exchange of violence"', *Early Medieval Europe*, 11 (2002), 1–18.

G. Herdt, *Third Sex, Third Gender: Beyond Sexual Dimorphism in Culture and History* (New York: Zone, 1994).

Intersections of Gender, Religion and Ethnicity in the Middle Ages, ed. C. Beattie and K. Fenton (London: Palgrave Macmillan, 2011).

B. A. Hanawalt, *Women and Work in Pre-Industrial Europe* (Bloomington, IN: Indiana University Press, 1986).

D. Kim, 'Rewriting liminal geographies: crusader sermons, the Katherine Group and the scribe of MS Bodley 34', *Journal of Medieval Religious Cultures*, 42 (2016), 56–78.

B. Lomer, *Hildegard of Bingen: Music, Rhetoric and the Sacred Feminine* (n.p.: VDM Verlag, 2009).

I. G. Marcus, 'Jews and Christians: imagining the other in medieval Europe', *Prooftexts*, 15 (1993), 209–226.

Masculinity in Medieval Europe, ed. D. M. Hadley (London: Longman, 1999).

L. Herbert McAvoy, *Medieval Anchoritisms: Gender, Space and the Solitary Life* (Cambridge: D. S. Brewer, 2011).

L. E. Mitchell, 'Gender(ed) identities? Anglo-Norman settlement, Irish-ness and the Statutes of Kilkenny of 1367', *Historical Reflections/Réflexions Historiques*, 37 (2011), 8–23.

J. L. Nelson, *Courts, Elites and Gendered Power in the Early Middle Ages: Charlemagne and Others* (Aldershot: Ashgate, 2007).

Derek G. Neal, *The Masculine Self in Late Medieval Culture* (Chicago: University of Chicago Press, 2008).

Janet L. Nelson, 'Monks, secular men and masculinity', in D. Hadley, ed., *Masculinity in Medieval Europe* (London: Longman, 1999): 121–142.

V. Neuberger, *Margery Kempe: A Study in Early English Feminism* (Berlin: Peter Lang, 1994).

H. J. Nicholson, 'Women's involvement in the crusades', in A. Boas, ed., *The Crusader World* (Abingdon: Routledge, 2016), 54–66.

K. Nowacka, 'Reflections on Christine de Pizan's "feminism"', *Australian Feminist Studies*, 17 (2002), 81–97.

The Origins of Racism in the West, ed. M. Eliav-Feldon, B. Isaac and J. Ziegler (Cambridge: Cambridge University Press, 2009).

Other Middle Ages: Witnesses at the Margins of Medieval Society, ed. Michael Goodich (Philadelphia, PA: University of Pennsylvania Press, 1998).

H. Paul, 'Editorial: women in economic and social history', *Economic History Review*, 68.2 (2015), E1–E17.

Kim Phillips, 'Warriors, Amazons and Isles of Women: medieval travel writing and constructions of Asian femininities', in *Intersections of Gender, Religion and Ethnicity in the Middle Ages*, ed. C. Beattie and K. A. Fenton (London and New York: Palgrave Macmillan, 2011), 183–207.

Postcolonial Approaches to the European Middle Ages: Translating Cultures, ed. A. J. Kabir and D. Williams (Cambridge: Cambridge University Press, 2005).

The Postcolonial Middle Ages, ed. J. J. Cohen (London: Palgrave Macmillan, 2001).

Race and Ethnicity in the Middle Ages, Special Issue of *Journal of Medieval and Early Modern Studies*, 31.1 (2001).

M. Rubin, 'The languages of late-medieval feminism', in *Perspectives on Feminist Political Thought in European History*, ed. T. Akkerman and S. Stuurman (London: Routledge, 1998), 34–49.

Single Life and the City, 1200–1900, ed. J. de Groot, I. Devos and A. Schmidt (Basingstoke: Macmillan, 2015).

M. Skinner, 'Benedictine life for women in central France, 850–1100: a feminist revival', in *Distant Echoes: Medieval Religious Women*, ed. J. A. Nichols and L. Thomas Shank (Kalamazoo, MI: Cistercian Publications, 1984), 87–113.

M. F. Stevens, 'London women, the courts and the "Golden Age": a quantitative analysis of female litigants in the 14th and 15th centuries', *The London Journal*, 37 (2012), 67–88.

What is Masculinity? Historical Dynamics from Antiquity to the Contemporary World, ed. J. A. Arnold and S. Brady (Basingstoke: Palgrave Macmillan, 2011).

C. Cannon Willard, *Christine de Pizan: Her Life and Works* (New York: Persea Books, 1984).

Glossary

alterity	The quality of being 'other'
consciousness raising	Raising awareness of gender inequality and ways to challenge it
constitutive	Creating an entity or idea
deconstruct	Read texts closely to explore how ideas are created by language, finding alternatives, challenging accepted interpretations

empirical	Based on known evidence, a confidence that the evidence gives a reliable picture
neologism	A novel term, a new word
patriarchal equilibrium	The ability of patriarchy to respond to women's advances by introducing or maintaining other restrictions
phallic	Relating to the male sex organ, and by extension male concerns
plurality	Result of **deconstruction** – the fact that categories such as 'men' can have multiple meanings and subcategories
polemicists	Those making provocative arguments designed to attack others
production	Work and its outputs, paid or unpaid
proto-industrialization	Period of transition when home-based, domestic labour (by men and women) became partly mechanized and requiring more capital than individual workers could raise
reproduction	Primarily, childbirth, but also choices relating to sex and contraception
socialization	Primarily, the upbringing of children and the ideas of 'normal' behaviours taught to them from an early age
social capital	Perceived importance or connections within a community

7

Studying Gender and Queering the Picture

I was struck, when starting to write this book, by how many conferences and meetings were held in the United Kingdom in 2014 and 2015 addressing questions such as 'Is gender still relevant?' (one that provoked online indignation amongst US colleagues), highlighting inequalities of gender and race in the academy, flagging up barriers to progression and conveying the sense that the exciting, risk-taking era of feminist gender scholarship was being closed down by increasing institutional pressures to demonstrate productivity. The anxiety seemed to come from two directions: first, the state of the profession, and a sense that women and younger researchers are losing out in an ever more aggressive, market-led higher education environment. In an era of austerity – jobs are scarce, funding for research is shrinking and casualization is common – 'safe' choices are more likely to be made in decisions who to fund, who to hire. But another reason for the anxiety, I suggest, is one that was highlighted by Gina Luray Walker in her keynote address to a 2014 conference called 'Gender, History and Society' at Winchester (UK) – the tendency of successive generations to forget – or never to be told of – their precursors, to have to reinvent the wheel of feminist or women's or gender-sensitive scholarship. And this is not just a problem that blighted Mary Hays' attempt in the eighteenth century to write a series of biographies of women in history (see Chapter 6).

One problem that is not being discussed is that of demographics. The scholars trained or starting their careers in the 1970s and 1980s, who challenged the male-centred framing of medieval culture (e.g. Pauline Stafford and Jinty Nelson in the United Kingdom, Susan Mosher Stuard, Caroline Walker Bynum, Joan Ferrante, Barbara Hanawalt in the United States), are now either retiring (albeit continuing to publish) or are no longer alive (e.g. Jo Ann McNamara, Angeliki Laiou and Gerda Lerner), and their pioneering work in raising new agendas and debates within the academy, worryingly, is becoming a footnote. Their very success in changing the conversation disguised the fact that it was often through their own personal energy, vision and scholarship that they built and maintained gender as a crucial historical approach. Those whom they trained, however, were still a minority in the academy, and perhaps did not realize that they would still have to fight so hard. And legacies matter – graduate students given the space to think critically in a supportive environment are likely to come up with entirely different perspectives to those (and they are many) working within more restrictive, patronage-based academic cultures where the authority of the 'professor' is still paramount, and conformity secures the postdoctoral opportunity. For students and instructors, courses that address gender past and present offer spaces that are inclusive and open, enabling and not closing down voices that challenge present-centred 'norms' of what counts as 'scholarly work'. Completing the book now, it has to be a matter of concern that the academy still accommodates senior scholars who attack both women and medievalists of colour for questioning the now unsustainable categories with which traditional medieval history has been shaped for over a century. It is more crucial than ever for currently senior scholars, the beneficiaries of that era of expansion, to ensure that they too create and maintain spaces (for themselves and others) to think, experiment and continue gender history's forward trajectory. The Society for Medieval Feminist Scholarship has been a beacon for this work.

Gender has indeed proven itself to be a useful category of analysis for medieval historians over the past thirty to forty years in which it has established itself in different forms. From the very basic equation of 'gender' with 'women', it has developed into a more sophisticated tool that enables us to explore not only the lives of women, but to include intersectional thinking about different social classes, religions, races, sexual activities (and identities) and bodily **impairments**. We have already met Crenshaw's idea of intersectionality in Chapter 1, an approach that focuses attention on multiple categories of analysis, rather than privileging just one. Arising from the concerns of black and minority ethnic scholars that race became invisible or overlooked

once a gendered (or class-based) light was shone on the evidence, intersectional work combines considerations of these categories all at once,
but also encourages the development of further refinements in terms of
reconstructing the experiences of particular groups or individuals. For
some, gender's elasticity, and ability to accommodate forms of disempowerment not primarily related to male or female identity, is a sign of
its lack of clarity and coherence. For others, such as Dorothy Kim, it has
offered the opportunity to put Crenshaw's intersectionality into practice
by blurring the boundaries of each category or group, and simply allow-
ing for a Middle Ages that is decidedly 'queer'.

Queering the Agenda

What exactly is meant by 'queer'? This is a debate in itself. What was a
previously homophobic term has been appropriated and repurposed by
gay, lesbian and transgender scholars to describe their alternative readings of medieval and modern sources and texts that have suppressed or
simply ignored the existence of alternative (but not for them) lifestyles.
In short, the queer is the not-normal, and in Judith/Jack Halberstam's
words, queer can encompass 'subcultural practices, alternative methods
of alliance, forms of transgender embodiment and … willfully eccen-
tric modes of being'. The point is then to raise the question of 'what is
"normal"'? Thinking queerly, therefore, forces researchers and students
to question what the assumed 'norm' might be. 'We do it because we've
always done it' is often a justification of the norm, but for historians this
is surely a challenge to be unpicked and questioned. The volume *Queering the Middle Ages*, published in 2001, and whose essays focused on both
literary and historical texts, did just this, offering the contributors the
opportunity to question the apparently stable categories used by scholars
to study medieval culture. One of its editors, Steven Kruger, emphasized
that queer theory had enabled the exposure of contemporary power relations in those categories, and gender historians were not exempt from his
criticism. For example, he suggested that creating scholarly work around
the term 'masculinity' implied a de-valued femininity and a negatively
charged 'effeminacy' as its opposites. The dominant framework assuming

heterosexuality as a norm at the same time marginalized and disavowed the possibilities of queer sexualities.

The queer approach took hold most strongly in readings of medieval literary work. Creative writings, after all, permit the exploration of categories that challenge and subvert societal attitudes, even as they then perhaps reinforce norms through a didactic or moralizing conclusion; queer readings of those texts – the theoretical approach that gives rise to the verb 'queering' – seeks to find the unsaid, unseen and yet present counter-narratives, the subversive voice of the author, or her/his protagonists, that suggest that the 'norm' is not so stable, not so policed, as the headline moralizing of the tale or account might have the audience believe.

Yet what constitutes a 'norm' in these circumstances then becomes less clear. It is not expressed in these terms by the medieval author, but captured in the work of Karma Lochrie. Her studies published from 1995 onwards were influential in challenging the **heteronormativity** of gendered approaches to the middle ages. The title of her *Heterosyncrasies: Female Sexuality when Normal Wasn't* expresses all possibilities in the term 'heterosyncrasies' and allows for forms of female sexuality that defy convention not (or not only) because they did not conform to the sorts of regulation we met in Chapter 4, but because they reveal how fragile those 'rules' were, that is there *was* no clear norm. Eve Kosofsky Sedgwick, whose work on homosociality was influential in early work on medieval masculinities (see Chapter 3), defines 'queer' as 'the open mesh of possibilities, gaps, overlaps, dissonances and resonances, lapses and excesses of meanings when the constituent elements of anyone's gender, of anyone's sexuality aren't made monolithically …'

Both authors' juxtaposing of gender and sexuality reflects the close, some might say defining, link with a thread of scholarship that cited queer (that is, non-straight) sexuality as one of the hidden and ignored, yet constantly present, elements of medieval society that only careful re-reading of source materials could reveal. But queer arguably goes beyond the body and sexuality. Even John Boswell, whose pioneering work on same-sex relationships we have already met in Chapter 3, suggested that 'no evidence supports the common idea that homosexual and heterosexual behavior are incompatible'. That is, he was questioning the very language and categories used in modern scholarship to express this 'common' idea, and thus engaging with scholars who sought to discard such labels and explore medieval sexuality (in this case) without preconceptions of what they would find. And this blurring – and rejection – of concrete categories represents a broader definition of 'queer' readings that see any kind of labelling as unnecessarily restricting readings of medieval sources to modern frameworks. At its most extreme, queer would reject the gender studies from which it emerged, along with theoretical approaches that privilege feminism, or race, or sexuality. It is an intersectional approach but (as Crenshaw intended) does not reify intersectionality *as an identity*. This is a challenging concept for many feminist scholars who see their own work as prefiguring and making space for queer theory to grow and flourish, and considerable work now exists trying to explore and perhaps even reconcile this apparent incommensurability.

Queer essentially derives its energy from a postmodern rejection of labels, but as German literary scholar Rüdiger Schnell pointed out, in an important article on the state of play as he saw it in 2012 (see Appendix), this meant that scholars claiming to work within queer studies had and have to accept that their *own* readings were/are entirely provisional, and without any more authority than the 'conventional' categories they sought to challenge. Schnell's article also revealed the clear fault line between the American scholarship that was the driver of queer readings from the early 1990s onwards, and European scholars who took longer to adopt this approach, or rejected it out of hand as 'a question not only of political, but of academic correctness' (here Schnell is quoting Andreas Kraß in an article of 2009).

Historians were slower to get on board with what was initially presented as a critical way of reading, that is, associated with literary studies rather than their own discipline. For historians, the negotiable readings proposed by queer theory fly very much in the face of history as an empirical discipline that still has some confidence in its ability to present a plausible picture of the medieval past based on assembling evidence. As Schnell points out (and I am dwelling on his article simply because it may be less accessible to Anglophone readers) 'queer studies' encompasses and imposes a single adjective – queer – for 'what earlier on in "conventional" medieval studies had been described and studied as "different, other, unusual, deviating from the norm, rejecting the norm, law-breaking, heretical or peculiar" … without having changed in fact whatsoever'. This worries him, and no doubt it also worries historians who have made careers in writing about the groups and categories (often referred to as 'marginal' members of medieval society, to which we shall return) that he lists, but in fact his criticism is deliberately provocative. He is not questioning an approach that is in fact intensely self-reflective and demands that each scholar take a long look at their own starting position and cultural attitudes, but lamenting that the label itself has become so prevalent, and covers so many *conflicting* strands, that it is losing its impact before it even takes hold. How to reconcile the identity politics of an LGBTQ+ movement that claims to queer the dominant, heterosexual narratives of history, for example, with a queer theory that rejects such identities as social constructs, and a radical feminism that denies transgender women are women? And, perhaps more pertinently from the present author's perspective, how to reconcile the notable advances of work undertaken by women's and gender historians, which undoubtedly has broken some of the more persistent moulds in medieval history, with a stance that in some quarters (see Kruger's critique above) sees such work as limited by its very focus on (often binary) gender? Yet it is worth persisting with a queer approach if what that means is a direct questioning (as gender studies also did and does) of how medieval historians have worked within a set of assumed and unquestioning frames and privileged not just the male and Christian, but also the European, white-skinned, heterosexual, able-bodied Middle Ages. By shining a light on these assumptions, the 'marginal', as presented by this very narrow range of medieval authors, in fact becomes rather less marginal, and the 'other', or 'Other' becomes distinctly problematic. Historians of women, for example, could discuss the minority of unmarried or never-married individuals and groups who had all too often been labelled as 'exceptional' (or even worse, 'masculine' by their contemporaries), but whose very existence might have been overlooked or elided from history because they did not conform. A queer approach allows the idea of exceptionality to vanish, in favour of studies that do not measure these lives against a predetermined medieval norm, but read them on their own terms. Margery Kempe's life might have been transgressively 'queer' – but her exceptionality rests in the *record* that exists of this life, rather than the all-too-human account of her frustrations that in places will seem almost familiar and 'normal', albeit with some startling and specific moments that defy categorization. The work of authors such as Judith Bennett, which has encouraged others to explore the lives of single and never-married women, enables a queerer, richer consideration of the possibilities open to women that is not confined to the views of medieval churchmen.

Although she does not use the term in her essay, Kathleen Biddick's critique of Bynum's *Holy Feast and Holy Fast* might be taken as an example of a queer reading (see Chapter 3). Biddick is uncomfortable with Bynum's category 'women mystics', arguing that gender histories 'need to be histories simultaneously of corporeal interiority and exteriority: sex, flesh, body, race, nature, discourse and culture'. For Biddick, Bynum had accepted as natural an undifferentiated Christian 'culture' that both enfolded but also marginalized the voices of her mystical women, and limited herself to this culture rather than working comparatively on food and flesh within other religions. There was also a tension between Bynum's own criticism of anachronistic, feminist approaches to the medieval texts whilst at the same time inserting herself and the readers of her book into the 'we' expressed by her medieval writers in order to hear the authentic voices therein. Bynum's category of the 'maternal', too, was questioned – was it as universal and trans historical as *Holy Feast and Holy Fast* apparently made it out to be? Biddick goes on to survey the reviews of the book, underlining the difficulty of trying to contain within one structural narrative the very different experiences of the individuals she was discussing. Ultimately, if queering Bynum made readers more attentive, it also sowed some doubts about what had already become a required student text on gender and women's history courses. Where Bynum had read maternal imagery, could there instead be alternative readings?

Beyond Different

We have moved a long way in this book from the apparently stable categories of male and female to a theoretical approach opening up all sorts of possibilities for understanding medieval biological, social and sexual identities. A lot of the work that is described as 'medieval gender' still deals in binaries: male/female, clerical/secular, straight/gay, Christian/non-Christian, black/white, able/impaired. This, as theologian Martin Stringer has commented, tends to fix 'difference' as a category of analysis, that is it creates opposing positions. A queer reading, however, picks up on the inherent diversity in medieval texts: the spectrum of possibilities around gender identity, even if some were frowned upon; the fluidity for most of the period in what it meant to be a Christian; a keener eye for what is not said. Binary categories are largely modern inventions: by engaging directly with medieval texts, it may be possible to strip away some of these long-held and invisible assumptions.

Queer thus offers intriguing possibilities to medieval historians for re-reading familiar medieval texts such as chronicles with a different focus. An analysis starting with gender already reads texts 'against the grain', and as an approach now raises few eyebrows. We have already begun to explore queerness in identifying how unstable the categories 'male' and 'female' become when understood to be points on a one-sex continuum. If we return to some of the examples already visited above, queer reading might ask whether transvestite saints were expressing a transgender identity in addition to, or rather than, simply trying to gain entry to a male environment, or whether their cross-dressing represented an entirely different mode of behaviour that is inadequately captured in the modern terms transgender, transsexual or even 'cross-dressing'. This is why this chapter offers not a source hunt at its conclusion, but a celebrated (within medieval gender studies at least) case of male-to-female cross-dressing whose record lends itself to any number of readings (as Ruth Mazo Karras, one of its original finders, will attest).

In 2018, therefore, students and teachers are faced with a bewildering array of approaches, and are told there is no 'right answer'. Gender is in fact now a highly fragmented label used to describe a wide spectrum of work. If 'gender' covers a broad range of materials, from empirical data collection on women's and men's lives to the critical re-readings of familiar texts informed by theoretical approaches borrowed from literary criticism and the social sciences, does it maintain any coherence or validity as an approach? I am cautiously optimistic: medieval studies over the past twenty years or so has become increasingly inclusive, with disciplinary boundaries mattering far less. Gender is increasingly applied to medieval *culture*, which means that collected volumes of essays are likely to include historians and literary specialists working alongside one another, but its questioning of categories undoubtedly contributed to this increased mingling of the disciplines. There is still plenty of room for gendered analysis. Recent work has included gender being used as a lens to explore time and memory in medieval culture, encompassing such themes as childbirth as a recurring memory event within families and communities, but also a time when a woman temporarily 'left' her religious community during a period of purification. Theories of race and monstrosity have been adopted and adapted to explore texts about crusading and conquest, where the viewpoint is often the victors' in such conflicts, but where their description of the enemy reveals as much about themselves as those they label 'Other'.

Post Gender?

But this fragmentation of meaning has other consequences: the structural approach of feminist historians, for whom a persistent and long-term patriarchy produced not only the oppression of women but also controlled the production of evidence, has been challenged and possibly even undercut by postmodern theories of contingency and textual production, a **poststructural** rejection of the over-arching narrative, and a **postfeminist** academy which questions the need to retain specifically female spaces. Gender as an analytical category is relational, not fixed: this is a postmodern position.

But if gender emerged from feminist work, does postfeminist thought threaten its continued validity? The Society for Medieval Feminist Scholarship tackled this question in both research and teaching terms in a special issue of *Medieval Feminist Forum* titled 'Are we post-feminist yet?' Is it to be understood in terms of time – the need for feminist struggle is over, and women are free to choose not only the lives their foremothers struggled for (the positive spin on the postfeminist age)? Many students that I have taught over the past twenty years have been intensely uncomfortable self-identifying as 'feminist' because they do not see the relevance of a past struggle to their own lives – are they, too, postfeminist? Or is being postfeminist having the right and ability to reject feminism as a political stance without damaging those advances already achieved? Kristin Anderson in fact highlights the way in which this complacency opens the way to a return to misogynist language and activity. Claiming that we live in a postfeminist age is used to permit often intensely misogynist men to claim it is fine to use language and behaviours that feminists would see as entirely inappropriate, but are justified on the grounds that they are legitimate responses to feminist arguments. Does being postfeminist mean that feminism no longer matters?

This raises an issue of intergenerational and interregional tensions. At the start of this book I identified 'waves' of feminism, and its gradual fragmentation into single-issue politics. Such an approach, of course, risks preferring one 'wave' over another, and these preferences might well be age-dependent (especially if the introduction of social media and technology into the mix excludes some colleagues from the fast-moving discussions because they have not made the transition to online debate). Yet another unsung and neglected process that gender history has fostered, with its rejection of exclusionary history and politics, is the easy and hierarchy-free dialogue between academic generations, in the Anglophone world at least. And yet self-proclaimed postfeminist work may present a serious challenge to the project of expanding gender history, since it is based on a mistaken assumption that feminist politics have achieved their goals and are no longer 'relevant' to contemporary academic practice. This might – *might* – be true of some western-style democracies (although not of their academies, if recent social media storms surrounding sexism and racism in the medieval academy are anything to go by). But it certainly is not universally applicable – and it belies an ignorance, or even arrogance, to close off a discussion simply because it seems out of date in one part of the academic world. At the same time, we should not assume that there is such a **historiographical deficit** between developed countries and the rest of the world without actively engaging with the academics working in the latter. It also begs the important question of power within the academy – who bosses these debates, who sets the agenda for what is and is not 'good' gender history? This is a particularly urgent question when the power of social media allows not only alternative viewpoints and queer perspectives to be expressed to a far more extensive audience than might have been the case even twenty years ago, but also permits those who still do claim authority within academic life to try – often in nakedly aggressive ways – to close down such debates. Online bullying is a toxic and career-damaging trend that the scholarly community would do well to call out and challenge every time.

Ultimately it is as well to remember the lesson that intersectionality and queer theory teaches all historians: the gendered practice of medieval history is not enough if, in focusing on binary gender relations, it ignores other dynamics at work such as class, racial prejudice (overt or implicit), the entrenched heteronormativity of medieval texts (and some prominent Faculty members), or an assumption of able-bodiedness as a standard when in fact permanent impairment of some kind was probably far more prevalent in medieval society than in the medicalized modern era. Gender opened the doors to study these and other groups, and those doors must remain open even if they have to have metaphorical feet placed in the way of their closure.

It should become clear from the issues discussed in this book that medieval historians and their colleagues in other disciplines are by no means agreed on how to approach gender. It might seem that the arguments being had about the lack of diversity within medieval studies sound rather like earlier arguments about the inclusion of neglected women. It might puzzle you to think that the author is 'dead' if we have a named author for some of the sources you've been hunting for. You might also wonder how reading queerly really helps and how it differs from reading with a gendered lens: both, after all, expose power relationships. The danger, as opponents of highly theoretical readings are quick to point out, is that we become so pre-occupied with this reflective style of reading that we convey nothing about lived realities of medieval life. I have read books on medieval culture where the author, duly drilled in these theoretical approaches, pauses every other sentence to clarify their intentions, understandings and assumptions – this does not make for engaging reading. Perhaps I'm just grumpy. Or perhaps the relative newness of the approach, and students keen to engage with it, results in overenthusiastic use (Schnell's point) that often gets wrapped up in complex terminology that only others 'in the know' can really understand and engage with.

Emerging from a long-standing concern with the under-represented and disempowered, medieval gender history retains its receptivity to new ideas, whilst rejecting the temptation to privilege one over the other as a sign of 'progress'. It has undoubtedly been refreshed and reoriented through its ongoing discussions with scholars of medieval literature, but the collapsing of boundaries between these two disciplines has perhaps led to the latter becoming a dominant voice in a field that possibly needs to recall, a century on from *Annales*, that 'total history' demands input from historians of *all* specialisms, social scientists and from experts in quantitative methods as well. This book has sought to bring together some of the ideas that have shaped the reading and re-reading of medieval texts, and then to encourage you to try them out. It is likely that you will have a preferred approach, and this might relate to perceived ease or difficulty in the approach under consideration. This is a live problem for students and their instructors. Gender historians, for whom a concern with power relations is central to their own research, have to engage critically with any theoretical stance that threatens to exclude more people than it includes. The language in which books on medieval culture are written *can* sometimes seem unnecessarily complex, particularly to students and general readers, but also to those not trained in the disciplines of philosophy and literature from which many theoretical approaches have emerged in the past 30–40 years. This textbook has been something of an **epistemological** study, exploring the **ontology** of working in medieval history in the past thirty years, and including the **hermeneutics** of medieval source materials. But don't just take my word for it – go and borrow a theory reader from the library too.

Source

'The questioning of John Rykener', published in the Internet Medieval Sourcebook at www.fordham.edu/halsall/source/1395rykener.asp.

Key Reading

K. J. Anderson, *Modern Misogyny: Anti-Feminism in a Post-Feminist Era* (Oxford: Oxford University Press, 2014).

K. Biddick, 'Genders, bodies, borders: technologies of the invisible', *Speculum*, 68.2 (1993), 389–413.

C. Walker Bynum, *Jesus as Mother: Studies in the Spirituality of the High Middle Ages* (Berkeley, CA: University of California Press, 1982).

J. Halberstam, *In a Queer Time and Place* (New York: New York University Press, 2005).

Intersections Between Feminist and Queer Theory, ed. Diane Richardson, Janice McLaughlin, Mark E.Casey (London: Palgrave Macmillan, 2006).

R. M. Karras and D. Lorenzo Boyd, '"Ut cum muliere": a male transvestite prostitute in 14th-century London', in Louise Fradenburg and Carla Freccero, eds, *Premodern Sexualities* (New York: Psychology Press, 1996), pp. 9–116.

R. M. Karras and T. Linkinen, 'John/Eleanor Rykener revisited', in *Founding Feminisms in Medieval Studies: Essays in Honor of E. Jane Burns*, ed. L. E. Doggett and D. E. O'Sullivan (Cambridge: D. S. Brewer, 2016), 111–124.

D. Kim, 'Divergent bodies and medieval studies', *In the Medieval Middle* (2014) www.inthemedievalmiddle.com/2014/08/divergent-bodies-and-medieval-studies.html [Accessed 1 July 2016].

K. Lochrie, *Heterosyncrasies: Female Sexuality When Normal Wasn't* (Minneapolis, MN: University of Minnesota Press, 2005).

Medieval Feminist Forum, 34 (2002): Special Issue 'Are we post-feminist yet?'

Queering the Middle Ages, ed. G. Berger and S. Kruger (Minneapolis, MN: Minnesota University Press, 2001).

M. D. Stringer, *Discourses on Religious Diversity: Explorations in Urban Ecology* (New York and London: Routledge, 2013).

Glossary

epistemology	Tracing how we know what we know, tracking the origins of ideas and knowledge
hermeneutics	Interpretation of texts, particularly but not exclusively biblical texts
heteronormativity	Assumption that male-female sexual activity is the norm
historiographical deficit	A judgement that history-writing in certain parts of the world is not 'up-to-date' or does not confirm to standards set by dominant regions, usually the English-speaking United States and Europe
impairment	A bodily injury or condition that may or may not affect actions
ontology	The lived reality, the state of being
postfeminist	Positive celebration of the advances made by feminism, leaving little room for further struggle, or negative attacks on feminists who insist there is some way to go to reach true equality
poststructural	Rejecting or modifying ideas that fundamental structures underpin all human social relations, and seeking instead to examine diversity of experience

Appendix:
Selected Works in Languages
Other than English

D. Bellacosa, *Il 'mundio' sulle donne in Terra di Bari dall'anno 900 al 1500* (Napoli, A. Forni, 1906) [*The 'mundium' over women in the region of Bari from the year 900 to 1500*].

G. Bohne, 'Zur Stellung der Frau im Prozess- und Strafrecht der italienischen Statuten', in *Gedenkschrift für Ludwig Mitteis* (Leipzig, Theodor Weicher, 1926) [The position of women in civil and criminal law of the Italian statutes].

Donne tra medioevo ed età moderna in Italia: ricerche, ed. G. Casagrande (Perugia, Morlacchi, 2004) [*Women between the Middle Ages and Modern Era in Italy*].

G. Dumas, *Santé et société à Montpellier à la fin du Moyen Âge* (Leiden: Brill, 2015) [*Health and society in Montpellier at the end of the Middle Ages*].

Glossa – Genos – Fylo, ed. Th.-S. Pavlidou, 2nd ed. (Thessaloniki: Institute of Modern Greek Studies, 2006) [*Language – Grammatical Gender – Social Gender*].

Handbuch Frauen- und Geschlechterforschung: Theorie, Methoden, Empirie, ed. R. Becker and B. Kortendiek (Berlin, Springer, 2008) [*Handbook of Women's and Gender Studies: Theories, Methods, Practice*].

S. Gäbe, 'Radegundis: sancta, regina, ancilla. Zum Heiligkeitsideal der Radegundsviten von Fortunate und Baudonivia', *Francia*, 16 (1989), 1–30. [Radegund: saint, queen, slave. On the ideals of holiness in the lives of Radegund by Fortunatus and Baudonivia.].

Geschlecht in der Geschichte: integriert oder separiert? Gender als historische Forschungskategorie, ed. A. Bothe and D. Schuh (Bielefeld, publisher transcript Verlag, 2014) [*Gender in History: integrated or separate? Gender as a category of historical research*].

L'histoire sans les femmes est-elle possible? ed. A.-M. Sohn and Françoise Thélamon (Rouen, Perrin, 1998) [*Is History without Women Possible?*].

Une histoire sans les hommes est-elle possible? ed. A.-M. Sohn (Lyons, ENS Editions, 2013) [*Is History without Men Possible?*].

S. Lebecq, A. Dierkens, R. Le Jan and J.-M. Sansterre, eds, *Femmes et pouvoirs des femmes à Byzance et en occident (VIe-XIe siècles)* (Lille: Centre de Recherche sur l'Histoire de l'Europe du Nord-Ouest, 1999) [*Women and the powers of women in Byzantium and the West*].

D. Lett, *Hommes et femmes au Moyen Âge: Histoire du genre XIIe-XVe siècle* (Paris, Armand Colin, 2013) [*Men and women in the Middle Ages: gender history 12th to 15th centuries*].

Margini di libertà: testamenti femminili nel medioevo, ed. M. C. Rossi (Verona, Cierre Edizioni, 2010) [*On the edges of freedom: women's wills in the Middle Ages*].

M. T. Guerra Medici, *I diritti delle donne nella società altomedievale* (Rome, Università di Roma, 1986) [*Laws on women in early medieval society*].

M. T. Guerra Medici, *L'aria di città: donne e diritti nella città medievale* (Rome, Feltrinelli, 1996) [*City air: women and laws in the medieval city*].

Les reseaux familiaux: antiquité tardive et Moyen Âge, ed. B. Caseaux (Paris, Peeters, 2012), a memorial volume for Angeliki Laiou and Evelyne Patlagean. [*Family resources: late antiquity and the Middle Ages*, papers in French and Italian].

E. Santinelli, *Des femmes eplorées? Les veuves dans la société aristocratique du haut Moyen Âge* (Lille, Presses Universitaires de Septentrion, 2003) [*Tearful Women? Widows in Early Medieval Aristocratic Society*].

R. Schnell, '*Queer studies* in der Mediävistik: Anspruch und Wirklichkeit' [2 parts], *Zietschrift für deutsche Philologie* 131 and 132 (2012 and 2013), 431–454 and 103–128.

Ser mujer en la ciudad medieval europea, ed. J. A. Solórzano Telechea, B. Arízaga Bolumburu and A. Aguiar Andrade (Longroño, Instituto de Estudios Riojanos, 2013) [*Being a Woman in the Medieval European City*].

Splendor Reginae: Passions, genre et famille. Mélanges en honneur de Régine Le Jan, ed. S. Joye, T. Lienhard, L. Jégou and J. Schneider (Turnhout, Brepols, 2015) [*The splendour of Régine [or, the Queen]: passions, gender and family*].

K. van Eickels, 'Männliche Zeugungsunfähigkeit im mittelalterlichen Adel', *Medizin, Gesellschaft und Geschichte*, 28 (2009): 73–95.

Journals Published in Languages other than English

Arenal: Revista de Historia de las Mujeres, founded 1994. No specifically medieval issue, articles from all periods represented in most volumes. Published by the University of Granada. www.ugr.es/~arenal/indices.php.

Cahiers de Civilisation Médiévale, founded 1958. Special double issue on women, no. 20.78–79, published in 1977.

DWF: Donnawomanfemme, founded 1975. www.dwf.it.

Duoda: Estudios de la Diferencia Sexual, founded 1990. Theoretically engaged, themed issues. Issue 9 explored Marguerite Porete (d.1310). Published by the University of Barcelona. www.ub.edu/duoda/web/es/revista.

GENDER: Zeitschrift für Geschlecht, Kultur und Gesellschaft, founded 2009. Predominantly focused on contemporary issues but early articles engaged with theoretical approaches.

Genesis: La Rivista della Società Italiana delle Storiche, founded 2002, succeeding *Agenda* which had published from 1990 to 1999. The gap is suggestive of the difficulties of finding an institutional place for women's studies in the Italian academy. Themed issues, some of which include medieval articles. www. societadellestoriche.it/.

Genre et histoire: la revue de l'Association Mnémosyne, founded 2007. Issue 3 was a special issue on *Les médiévistes et l'histoire du genre en Europe* [*Medievalists and the history of gender in Europe*]. http://genrehistoire.revues.org.

Storia delle Donne, founded 2005.

Index

Note: Medieval persons are listed by their first name; modern authors are listed surname, forename.

Lightning Source UK Ltd.
Milton Keynes UK
UKHW022233180222
398910UK00010B/2410